"Bach has taken a complicated subject and deftly simplified it for the layman."
— Los Angeles Herald Examiner

"Extremely accessible, with specific exercises outlined to make the process doable and even enjoyable."
— Publishers Weekly

"Some good tips and a reintroduction to some of the more interesting inhabitants of your interior."
— Charlotte Observer

THE INNER ENEMY

HOW TO FIGHT FAIR WITH YOURSELF

DR. GEORGE R. BACH
AND LAURA TORBET

B

BERKLEY BOOKS, NEW YORK

FOR

the patients, students, colleagues,
Institute staff members, and friends
who shared the workings of their
Inner Enemy with us in trust.

THE INNER ENEMY

Foreword

IN 1945, while working as a psychotherapist with my first group of adult patients at the Western Reserve University clinic in Cleveland, Ohio, I was impressed and puzzled by their tendency to be either too hard or too easy on themselves. This initial impression has been borne out through nearly four decades of clinical practice. As I look back on my work with over four thousand individuals I cannot recall a single case that did not involve to some degree an inner struggle between extremes of self-love and self-loathing. It is as true today of the sophisticated, successful people I have treated in Hollywood as it was then of the young, more naïve patients at the university clinic.

As a therapist, I became involved in the attempt to extricate them from their unproductive struggles, and would tailor their treatment according to whether the individual maladjustment leaned toward self-esteem or self-denigration.

Working to assist these patients, I encountered a strong resistance to making a change for the better. This frustrating and paradoxical reaction motivated me to search for the causes of such baffling behavior. And that is how after years research I discovered the twerp, the inner demons, responsible for the confusion in self-assessment and for distorting and disturbing the balance of self-praise and self-criticism. In previous books (*The Intimate Enemy, Pairing, Creative Aggression,* and *Stop! You're Driving Me Crazy!*) I have explained how such deep-seated discontent expresses itself in destructive ways in the context of intimate relationships.

In this book I am happy to share and explain my methods for dealing with these inner demons at the source: within ourselves. *The Inner Enemy* provides tools for the individual to help himself maintain the inner balance of positive and negative voices.

GEORGE R. BACH

Acknowledgments

MANY PEOPLE HAVE contributed profoundly in various forms to the production of this book and to the psychological research on which it is based. We would like to mention first the many people who came to the Bach Institute in West Hollywood, California, and the individuals who attended the Inner Enemy lectures and workshops at the University of California, at Santa Barbara City College, and at other schools around the country and in Europe. Their willingness to try out on themselves the techniques described in this book in their private struggles with their own Inner Enemy provided validation and the motivation to make our approach available to the public, beyond the college campus.

Our families deserve special thanks for the supportive, caring environment they provided during the writing of this book. We would like to make special mention of Dr. Roger Bach, George Bach's son, colleague, and continual consultant on this project, and of his other children, Stephanie, Claudia, Felicity, his daughter-in-law, Sheila, his son-in-law, Steve Harrison, his wife, Peggy-Jane. Everybody in this large family deserves credit for their insights and valuable advice.

From start to finish Dr. Herbert Goldberg offered his professional expertise as a clinical psychologist, provided objective and constructive criticism, and most helpfully tried out our techniques on his own students and patients. We are much in his debt. Special credit is also due to Professor Lewis Yablonsky, who helped Dr. Bach at UCLA and at the Bach Institute by developing special psychodramatic procedures which in trial runs were found useful in raising our subjects' awareness of how their Inner Enemy hinders them in their quest for self-actualization.

Going over the list of other helpers may be tedious for the reader, but it expresses the heartfelt gratitude of the authors. Other colleagues and friends who made valuable contributions include Dr. Seymore Fessbach, Dr. Zev Wanderer, Dr. Vance Kondon, Michelle Claire, Dr. Cedric Emery, Barbara Branstetter, Dr. Hartmuth Scharfe, Dr Robert Aikman, Dr. Susan Campwell, Lynn Chiles, Dr. Simon Beaudet, Dr. Bruce Parsons, Dr. Eric Field, Dr. Robert Benedetti, Sascha Schneider. Luree Nicholson, Dr. Bach's assistant for many years, steadfastly believed that the theory and methods of "creative aggression" could and should be applied not only to interpersonal actions but to the inner, intrapersonal realm as well. Luree's firm encouragement in this direction helped to get this book project started years ago. Becky McMurry found several research subjects for us, Julie Reed suggested variations in the body-image exercises, and Ron Deutsch helped in the development of "self-crazymaking" techniques. Dr. Harold Greenwald, President of the Professional School for Humanistic Studies in San Diego, California, provided an educational laboratory in which the theoretical principles described in this book could be practiced and their validity tested out.

Finally, special thanks to Hap Hatton and very special thanks to Peter Morrison.

Contents

PART III: HOW TO FIGHT FAIR WITH YOURSELF

Introduction

THIS BOOK IS the closure to Dr. Bach's cycle of books on aggression, which began with publication of *The Intimate Enemy* in 1974 and continued with *Pairing, Creative Aggression,* and *Stop! You're Driving Me Crazy!*

It attacks the sad and pervasive phenomenon of aggression against the self: the archenemy of self-realization, of interpersonal relationships—and of the psychiatric community. The Inner Enemy is the last barrier—the real barrier—to people's desire to lead satisfying lives, to realize the growth potential of the organism.

The Inner Enemy seems incongruous with the individual's desire to get ahead, to be who he dreams of being. Yet in spite of a conscious desire to succeed, he fails, day by day, little by little, usually by his own hand. The negative, self-critical propaganda of the entrenched Inner Enemy drowns out the voices of growth and self-worth that must be allowed to speak and to have impact. For the Inner Enemy is a spoiler, a vicious and elusive demon who can cause ruin and despair, who holds the individual in his grip by instilling fear and doubt. A life lived at the mercy of the Inner Enemy—to whatever degree—is a tragic one, for it is a life shortchanged. At the extreme the unresolved inner conflict leads to terror and madness. The battle for power, for recognition, among the inner voices is the ultimate human conflict.

The course and tenor of one's life are determined by how well one copes with the Inner Enemy. Though elusive and often incomprehensible, the Inner Enemy must be confronted if the individual hopes for success. Fortunately, the very process of taking responsibility for managing the Inner Enemy, for employing the self-help strategies detailed herein, is itself an effective weapon for changing self-defeating behavior.

GEORGE R. BACH
LAURA TORBET

Los Angeles, 1982

I

WHO DO YOU THINK YOU ARE?

1

The Inner Enemy

Going on inside all of us, all the time, is an incessant dialogue. This Inner Dialogue is the way western man thinks: It is a dialectical process in which two or more inner voices debate every little issue—from whether one looks gorgeous or ugly in the bathroom mirror in the morning, to whether one should buy a station wagon or a sports coupé, to the big debates such as, "What is the meaning of life?" or "Am I doing the right thing?" In fact, what we consider our "self" is really a group of voices, or selves, in constant conversation, whether consciously or unconsciously, overtly or covertly. This conversation takes place in the form of dialogues, debates, dreams and day-dreams, wishes, longings, reminiscences, feelings and ideas.

Not everyone is tuned in to his Inner Dialogue. Some people have no interest in it; others have no access to theirs, for much of their Inner Dialogue never rises above the unconscious. But most people are aware that they are always thinking on *some* level, even if they can't always pin down their thoughts or make sense of what's going through their heads. What they don't realize is that there is not just one person—a monolithic Me—talking in there, but many Me's. They fail to see the obvious: that the self which says you look wonderful in that green dress can't be the same self that says in the next breath that no one will be interested in talking to you at the party. Or that the supportive voice which congratulates you on making that difficult phone call can't be the same voice that *neglects* to tell you (as it usually does) to watch out for the low shelf when you stand up from the phone. Or that the inner voice telling you it's time to have a baby is not the one which says, "But then you'll never write that master's thesis."

Once we try to tune in to the Inner Dialogue and bring it into consciousness, we can start to pick out the different voices (or thinkers, or parties, or subselves) and see who they are. We become aware of the constant, pervasive, ongoing weeding-out process by which we live our lives. We note the complexity and overlap of the many voices, we are surprised by the many forms in which we communicate with ourselves. We are struck by the seemingly contradictory nature of the voices: Can the person who craves tomato soup and Saltines be the same one who just conjured up the image of the ice cream sundae he or she had last Thursday? Can the same person have a sublime insight cross his mind, even as he tells a foolish joke? Can a morbid thought coexist with a ridiculous one?

Jake became very aware of his conflicted inner voices as he planned his fall vacation: "First I planned to go to the Grand Canyon. Then I had a dream about a deserted beach. Out of the blue I remembered a visit I made long ago to Aspen. Then I was struck by a picture of Japan in a bookstore window. Further, I had three or four voices opposed to any trip at all. I had another dream—this one of a skiing accident. To add to my confusion, a feeling of self-indulgence came over me as I read the tour folder. I found myself discussing with a friend the importance of meeting work obligations.

There were many voices that had something to say about that trip."

When we start listening to the Inner Dialogue to find out how we think and feel about ourselves, we soon understand the literal meaning when we say, "I'm of two minds."

Then it becomes apparent that some voices are stronger, more talkative, more glib and persuasive, more prominently placed than others. We are more familiar with some voices than with others, and we pay attention to some more than others. In fact, certain voices—especially the self-supporting ally voices which try to praise and encourage us—rarely speak above a whisper or are routinely shouted down. Some seem to stay out of certain kinds of arguments, and join the debate only when they have a special ax to grind.

A young advertising copywriter notices that when he is working, most of the voices are supportive and useful. They reassure him that he is doing a good job, they supply good ideas and information. When he starts to worry, they tell him not to be anxious. When doubts surface they are quickly overcome by voices of reason that remind him of past successes.

Then he gets ready to leave work and meet his date for a drink. Suddenly he realizes he's exhausted and has a slight headache; his stomach feels queasy. He remembers an important phone call he has to make and wonders if he shouldn't beg off till tomorrow. He has been very comfortable in those corduroys and that V-necked sweater all day. Now suddenly they look rumpled, and he thinks maybe the dark blue is too unexciting, undistinguished. When he looked in the mirror this morning, the phrase "handsome devil" came to mind. Now he is sure his date only goes for really good-looking men. Who are these negative voices? How come they left him alone while he worked? And where are his inner friends now?

Sometimes the Inner Dialogue is calm, rational, and to

the point. Sometimes it keeps quiet while you get your work done or watch a movie, and confines itself to appropriate, useful comments or to the job at hand. At other times it rants and screams and jumps around in apparent chaos, making work, or watching a movie, impossible. It can be evasive: At times the voices scramble off into corners, speaking in whispers, playing games; you feel you "don't know your own mind." Sometimes the Inner Dialogue cajoles; sometimes it praises. At other times it taunts, or whines, or accuses. Sometimes it tells the same boring story over and over and over, for years on end, an interminable round robin of "Isn't it time you quit this dead-end job?" or "You should have married Elena" or "You're much too fat, if only you had a little willpower, you'd lose those ten pounds, you look terrible in this dress . . ." and so on. Our Inner Dialogue is our very own soap opera. Sometimes it interests us, or it may bore us to tears. Sometimes it scares us half to death.

For what happens too often is that the negative, teasing, naysaying, critical, vindictive, hurtful voices get the upper hand. They win out in the constant battle to be heard and end up making the decisions, informing our actions, pushing aside the positive, friendly, supportive, growth-directed voices. When this happens we turn against ourselves: "That was sheer stupidity of me to leave my wallet in the hotel room." We do things we know are no good for us: "There's no reason why I shouldn't celebrate with a few drinks. I worked hard for this raise." We lead ourselves down dark and destructive alleys. We do and say things to ourselves that no one else would ever dare to say or probably even think of; we do to ourselves what we would never do unto others. We become weakened by the battering of negative voices, unable to function at the top of our skills, and emotionally blunted.

The fact is that most people, in big and little ways, every day and every hour, act in self-destructive ways far more harsh and self-punitive than anything they are likely to encounter on the meanest of streets. They act toward themselves in ways that make violence, natural catastrophe, inflation, and the hazards of air pollution pale in comparison. In short, they terrorize themselves. The Inner Enemy is their own worst enemy.

"Whenever I receive a compliment, I blurt out without thinking: 'Oh, it was nothing' or 'I didn't pick out this dress.' It's not true, and I secretly love the praise and usually (I think) I secretly believe it, but I can't seem to stop myself."

"In the last year, I have left original drafts of my project proposals on the subway three times. I work so hard developing the concepts, planning, budgeting. Then I take them home, usually the last weekend before they're due, to polish and type them. Each time I tell myself to be careful. Each time I remind myself to make a photocopy to leave at the office. Each time, *I don't do it.* Leaving the stuff on the subway I can rationalize some way—I'm usually tired, tense, worried about how the project will be received, concerned about the validity of the ideas. But why don't I make a copy, especially since I recognize the problem? It's so self-punishing."

"I'm finally catching on to why I can't seem to find a guy to settle down with—which I really want to do. I know I'm fussy, and I'm not about to just marry anybody, but still . . . I went out with a film director the other night, who several of my friends had raved about, and I was distracted all evening by, of all things, his *eyebrows*. They were real heavy and bushy, and they seemed to cover his whole face. I felt mesmerized and repelled and couldn't keep my attention on the conversation. The next day when my girlfriend Kate called to ask how my date had been, I immediately replied, 'Well, OK, I guess, but he had these *awful* eyebrows.' Well, Kate really lit into me, pointing out that over the last six months I'd rejected various otherwise suitable prospects on the first date because: one was balding, one wore awful 'square' suits, one ate too much junk food, one voted for Reagan, and one admitted to having a messy apartment. She made me see how it's me who's keeping myself at a distance, me who's finding ways to reject, me who's sabotaging my chances to get what I want. And I've been doing this for years."

Becoming aware of the Inner Dialogue, encouraging fair debate leading to decisions which reflect our own best interests, are crucial, *for the outcome of the Inner Dialogue determines the course of our lives.* It makes the difference between success and failure, pleasure and pain, self-esteem and self-loathing.

Most people are genuinely concerned with leading meaningful lives, lives of credit to themselves and those they love and care about. The urge to fulfillment, to a larger existence, to growth and forward movement, is present in everyone. Yet so often people find—at some times more than others and in some areas of their lives more than others—that they get in their own way. They block the good feelings in favor of negative ones. They make the wrong decisions over and over again. Sometimes they are small decisions—a woman has a habit of ordering something on a restaurant menu and then realizes she wanted something else. But at other times the choices people make have the power to change their lives—and too often for the worse. A couple keeps saying they want to take it easier, move to the country, lead a simpler life. But then she is tempted by another job she can't pass up; he sees a new car he must have. They don't find time to pursue their dream. They get too busy to realize what's happening to it, and then wonder why they're still so unhappy. Another man pairs up with someone who is mean and critical of him, or who doesn't appreciate his talents, his loving qualities, or whose values are very different from his. Yet he chooses the same person over and over and over, in different clothing; he keeps thinking that the new relationship makes sense at the time, that this one is different. Who are these voices that drown out our own best interests? Why do we give them such attention? Such power? Who's running our lives anyway?

Tuning in to the Inner Dialogue is not easy. Much of the conversation goes on unconsciously; the Inner Enemy is happy to keep it that way, happy to have you confused and mystified and feeling generally miserable. When negative voices are in power, they are in a position to affect the actions and decisions by which we live. Leave it to your friends to step up and pat you on the back and tell you you're wonderful. The Inner Enemy is happy to hide and torment you in devious, hard-to-pin-down ways, eager to overrule the opinions of friendly ally voices. It doesn't want publicity. It doesn't want to be found out.

But the Inner Enemy must be uncovered, for as long as it is unconscious—beyond your range of vision, hearing, and understanding—it has the power to control and torture you. Once you bring those negative voices out into the light for closer scrutiny, they lose much of their terror, their impact is blunted, their power to surprise is greatly diminished. You see them more clearly, understand more how to cope with them.

The reluctance of the Inner Enemy to surface must not be underestimated. Anyone who has tried to free-associate—to say what comes to mind as it comes to mind—in psychoanalysis, in therapy, or with a friend, is aware of the terrible censorship and selectivity we impose on ourselves, the barriers we erect between our desire to know ourselves and the resistance and fear that accompany it. All confrontations are difficult, but a confrontation with ourselves, a falling out with our own inner voices, could tear us apart. It seems safer to learn to live with the Inner Enemy, to back off from confrontation. Or to deny the existence of the Inner Enemy, or its power over us. And remain anxious. And unfulfilled.

Many people are aware, if only dimly, of how they get in their own way. They are aware of the contradiction between the self that wants to grow and move forward and the self that keeps pulling the rug out from under them. They wonder, dream, and daydream about what they could do "if only . . ."

This book is about the *if only*.

The Inner Enemy is the *if only*. The Inner Enemy is those things *inside* people that hold them back. And it is within people's power not to lick the Inner Enemy, not to join it, but to learn to live with it in an atmosphere of fair debate and fair play, of equal time for inner friends as well, and to learn to turn these negative energies and anxieties into more creative and self-benefiting channels.

You cannot be rid of the Inner Enemy, but you can greatly reduce its power to terrorize and undermine you. If you can handle the Inner Enemy, the self-crazymaking, self-inhibiting, self-critical forces, you can handle any outer enemy. As you bring the Inner Enemy out of hiding and into the light, you will be able to make choices—reasoned, positive choices—from among many voices and possibilities, which will allow you to lead the more fulfilled life which beckons so tantalizingly just out of reach.

2

Aggression Against the Self: You Call This Hedonism?

WHO IS THE Inner Enemy and what nourishes it? Why is it saying those terrible things about you? In the simplest terms the Inner Enemy is the *uncreative* focus of our anxieties. *It is our anger turned inward on ourselves.*

Much has been written in recent decades about interpersonal aggression: conflict in families, between spouses, in the community. Anger is acceptable in polite company these days; the suppression or denial of anger is no longer considered to be the correct therapeutic approach. Many people have learned to use their anger constructively in their dealings with others. They have learned to confront their spouses, to deal fairly with their children, to make their voices heard in the community. They have taken assertiveness training or studied martial arts. Yet they remain unaware of the hostile, hurtful ways in which they turn their anger against themselves. This observation germinated the idea for this book: It has been Dr. Bach's experience, in his many years of practice as a specialist in aggression and its constructive uses, that interpersonal aggression can be worked out far more quickly and easily than anger against the self, which seems to be particularly difficult and intractable.

When we do read about aggression against the self, it's usually about its extreme and obvious manifestations: alcoholism, drug abuse, sadomasochism, criminal behavior, psychosomatic illness, suicide. What often gets glossed over in popular literature is the pervasive, everyday, slow torture—hard to identify and hard to acknowledge—that characterizes the ways in which people turn against themselves. What is overlooked or not acknowledged is the extent to which their self-hate influences their thoughts and actions:

> They get to work late, every day.
> They say something they don't mean to someone who counts—a lover, a child, a boss.
> They call themselves names and taunt themselves for every imagined mistake or act of negligence.
> They waste time with people who are negative and unproductive, or on time-wasting activities.
> They worry—about disease, about whether anyone loves them, about where their children are, about whether there will be an economic depression.

Many people back off in horror from this idea. They don't like to talk about it. They are more conscious of that part of themselves they consider "healthy"—the positive, self-supportive, growing, striving person that lives up to their expectations. They are comfortable with that person and with that self-image. "I'm not self-defeating. I don't punish myself," they say. "I look out for myself very well; I'm probably a little on the selfish side, if anything." They are often literally *un*conscious of, *un*aware of—and unwilling to accept—the negative, subversive, hostile anti-self. For the whole idea seems ludicrous; it couldn't possibly be true. Aren't we after all supposed to be very self-involved (narcissistic is today's catchall term), pleasure-seeking hedonists? Are we not primarily concerned with success, material comfort, getting ahead? Isn't most of what we do self-serving, even selfish? Isn't it human nature to act at all times in our own best interest?

Rarely is this theory of human nature questioned, but it is patently wrong. Of course, all sorts of evidence can be mustered to demonstrate how self-centered we are. Do we not spend more money on discos than on day care? More time with our golf buddies than with our children? Is our neighborhood not filled more with crime than with concern? Is not terrorism, local and global, the stuff of the daily news?

OK, but then how do we explain the other side of the coin? One has only to look closely at human behavior to see that we often act against our own self-interest, sometimes in subtle and teasing ways, at other times brutally and using a blunt instrument. How else to explain the fact that when things are going particularly well, we panic or get sick, or have bouts of insomnia, or are plagued by nightmares? Why do we suddenly have some easily avoidable household accident, or discover a problem in a previously smooth-sailing area of our lives? Why does good fortune have us looking over our shoulder, or drive us to drink a bit more than usual? Why at times are we simply unable to function? What or who is it whispers to us that it's all right to eat the extra brownie, taunts us that we will never win this tennis match, looks back at us in the mirror and declares that we are terribly ugly or unattractive? Who is it that constantly goads us to do more, never gives us enough credit for our accomplishments, lays it on thick with premonitions of failure? Certainly not our friends, or our loved ones, or even our teachers or employers. This punitive, destructive creep is our own Inner Enemy. It is the little twerp inside us who never lets up: "Who do you think you are," it asks, "walking upright, trying to be successful, to be content, to be loved and lovable, trying to have a good time? You've got a lot of nerve. I'll show you." What the outside world dishes out is small potatoes compared with the everyday slow torture of self-terrorization.

The twerp-free individual is a rarity. Very few people escape the clutches of the Inner Enemy, though many try and deny its presence or power. Even John McEnroe, at the top of his profession, playing in the finals at Wimbledon, browbeats himself, calling himself "stupid" over and over again, even hitting himself with the racquet. The twerp has become part of his arsenal. Also, in some people it takes unique subversive forms, making it hard to recognize—and easy not to admit to. There are those who resist recognizing its existence. These people are usually the kind who work very hard to keep their lives on an even keel, and who present themselves to the world as "together," "on top of everything."

"One night during dinner with eight people in attendance, we were talking about the Inner Enemy and how each of us could see ways in which his or her own twerp operated. One woman swore that she had no Inner Enemy and was never plagued by negative thoughts and self-doubt. And, indeed, it was easy enough to believe on the surface, because she was very beautiful and always seemed to be in a very even mood. Then later on during dinner when the topic of conversation had shifted, she regaled the dinner table with the story of how she taught herself to faint to get attention, and how she mimicked the symptoms of her friends who had tonsillitis for the same purpose. In fact, she did it so well that she had to go to the hospital and have her tonsils removed, even though she tried to convince her family and doctors that she was really all right."

Even with some evidence to back it up, the idea of our own self-defeating behavior is hard to swallow. It goes against the grain of everything we like to believe about human nature. In fact, most people have all sorts of reasons and rationalizations to explain why things haven't been going right for them, why they haven't accomplished all they would have liked. Marianne couldn't get any painting done because the phone kept ringing all day. Allan lost the golf game because his partner kept talking every time he would go to hit the ball. Elly couldn't go back to school because her husband didn't want her to be out when he got home. It is much easier to lay the blame at the hands of others, or to blame bad luck, or to blame society in general—the cold, cruel world. But much of the damage is done by our own hand.

If it is still hard to see how the Inner Enemy manifests itself, it's not surprising. Its ways and means are legion—varied, subtle, shifting:

"I thought I'd made great progress with the Inner Enemy and had gotten under control many of the self-sabotaging things I used to do: drink too much, alienate colleagues, worry constantly about my heart, bicker with my wife. But now that my life is running quite smoothly—and as a result of my own hard work, I'm proud to say—I've been having awful nightmares—disasters in which friends are involved, or I lose a job, or my wife gets angry and leaves."

"I had to turn down a job promotion because the new position required me to make regular presentations to employee groups and I could not overcome my terror of public speaking. Whenever I thought about it, all I could imagine was the worst-case scenario: I'd say the wrong things, I'd stutter, I'd forget things, my slip would show. That was four years ago, and it's only gotten worse; somehow I should have forced myself to go through with it. This failure has been a torment to me; and of course I've let it go too long. I'll never try to better my career position now."

* * *

"I go through a cycle: First, I look around for evidence that my wife doesn't love me, then I confront her with the evidence. In the ensuing argument I make it impossible for her to defend herself. At first, she was sympathetic to me when I did this. Now it makes her mad and makes her feel I don't appreciate her. So then we get in a fight; then I go off feeling bad for what I did, knowing it wasn't true—but not able to admit it to her. Slowly, of course, it's eroding her trust in me and her willingness to be open with me."

"Often when I'm having a real good time—laughing, forgetting my troubles for a change—a strong feeling of dread will come over me, like a pressure on the back of my neck, and my skin tingles. Yet there's no apparent reason for this feeling."

"My 'best friend' is always criticizing me—about how I look, about not paying enough attention to her, about the way I keep my apartment, about all the sugar I eat. She rarely has anything nice to say. I tend to dismiss as less valid the opinions of other friends who are much more supportive."

"I must call myself some name or another—stupid, fool, lazy, lunkhead—at least twenty times a day."

"I've lost my glasses four times already this year."

"I never miss a deadline on my monthly column, but it always involves staying up for two nights straight, drinking too much coffee, worrying, missing seeing friends or going to the theater, feeling sick and run-down afterward, and feeling bad about myself, too."

"I hate to be alone. I can never think of anything to do, so I worry and become anxious or just sleep. To avoid being alone, I'll go out anywhere, with anyone, to parties, bars, bowling, fishing—never anything that interests me. And I end up dating women, and sleeping with women, who bore me to tears. I end up wasting time and money and feeling worse afterward."

"For years I've wanted to take tennis lessons, but each time I have an opportunity I find some reason why I can't do it now—not enough time or money, or I don't like the pro or the courts."

"I'm so self-conscious about my weight that I avoid going to bed even with men I care about. Yet I don't lose the weight—and it's only ten pounds."

People pay a high price for their self-punitive ways in the pleasure and accomplishments they deny themselves. Somehow it is more comfortable to keep themselves in check—in constant terror and stress—than to confront the Inner Enemy and move forward. There is safety in the status quo, in the fear of the anger or of the vituperative tide that might be unleashed, the fear of admitting the loss of love they still crave. They would rather take the rap for being narcissistic, hedonistic, and self-indulgent than admit that another body of evidence exists that contradicts the notion. In fact, the very sheepish way in which they browbeat themselves about their self-centeredness is evidence of the opposite: They are really feeling guilty about many of the pleasures they allow themselves, as if they don't deserve them. They are ashamed that they're not happy with all they've got; they are only too glad to make themselves miserable with self-criticism. Not that the Me Decade didn't have its excesses—or more correctly, its misdirections—but are people not entitled to some of the good things in life, with no strings (such as guilt) attached?

What happens when people turn against themselves is that they lose those instincts that move them forward or help them grow. In psychological terms, they become neurotic. They become corrupted by their fears. And their greatest fear is that they will lose themselves. They are terrified that if they really fight with that sneaky hidden enemy, they will alienate it and hence a part of themselves; they will tear themselves asunder. It is one thing to alienate a spouse, a friend, a parent, but who is left if there is a rift within oneself? So when they try and tune in to the Inner Dialogue, they are fearful of clarity and have a hard time pinning the voices down—the messages are garbled and elusive; there seems to be an unintelligible babble; they feel stressed and anxious.

The fight with ourselves is the hardest fight of all. It is a battle fought in slow steps, in which long-ingrained habits of negative thinking must be redirected. But it is the most rewarding, for it is here that the proper channeling of aggressive impulses has the most enduring and beneficial results. It is in learning to fight fair with ourselves that we shed irrational fears, erode barriers that keep us rooted in unproductive patterns. It is a fight in which the aggression can be rerouted to the service of our needs and dreams.

3

Safe and Sane Self-Interest

PERHAPS IT SEEMS strange to be writing a book about the Inner Enemy—about self-realization and the inner life—now that the Me Decade has officially been declared over. Nowadays anything that smacks of self-centeredness is suspect. People are aware—and unreasonably ashamed—of the excesses and misdirections of too much self-involvement and too little other-involvement, or of too much self-actualization and not enough other-actualization.

In the quest for self-improvement, for a reprieve from fears or from limited lackluster lives, many people went too far, often in unproductive directions. Sidetracked, isolated, they came to realize that they had not found the answer or the satisfaction they were seeking in what started out as a serious, well-intentioned quest. Now they realize that becoming stronger and more perfect is only a partial answer to their needs, that they must confront, rather than try to escape, their inner demons, and they must reinforce and expand their connections to others.

Today self-actualization is pooh-poohed and narcissism

has become a dirty word. The psychiatric community has (quite rightly) shifted from enjoinment to "do your own thing" to "do unto [or, better, *with*] others." The self-interest backlash is quite strong. Now people criticize themselves harshly for being too self-involved, for wanting to know themselves and find ease in their lives.

The problem is not so much that it is wrong to be introspective or seek personal fulfillment, but that people too often go about it wrong, in ways that tend to alienate them not only from others but from their true selves.

Their misdirected quest has inadvertently strengthened the Inner Enemy; under such circumstances the Inner Enemy has a field day. In an age of self-actualization, the twerp gets riled. Threatened, it acts up more than ever. The Inner Enemy doesn't want to see us escape its snare, and unless we understand how it works, unless we give it due respect, we won't escape. The more rolfing and *est* and vitamins we take, the farther we jog, the more cars we buy, the greater distance we try to put between our self-defeating mechanisms and the self that is trying to be successful, the more violent the Inner Enemy will be.

It makes excessive self-concern a doubtful enterprise, unless . . .

Unless we learn to be *properly, sanely* self-interested. Unless we take the Inner Enemy into account and see what part it plays in our self-improvement plans. Unless we learn to distinguish good from bad, proper from improper, safe from sorry self-interest. Unless we get to know, and encourage, the ally voices to have a fair say in our judgments and decisions. And unless we give self-interest its proper place and acknowledge that self-care and knowledge are the basis for other-care and knowledge.

To become an adult one must make the transition from being respected by others to self-respect—and from being rejected by others to self-rejection. Unless people are able to undertake and manage themselves, no amount of verification from the outside world will equal the judgment of their inner voices. As long as self-improvement—jogging and meditation and cooking classes—is focused on making others love and respect them or on blotting out the disturbing inner voices, or is used as a defense against the lack of love from others or to make them feel superior or autonomous, nothing will be able to override inner feelings of doubt and worthlessness.

So we must take a new look at self-interest—at what it means, at its goals and ingredients, to learn about how it differs from the isolated and autonomous self-interest of the discredited Me Decade.

There are many positive arguments for self-interest. First of all, we are entitled to it: It benefits not only us but those around us. We have to be at ease with what we have pejoratively labeled self-involvement and accept that the pursuit of the Inner Enemy is a worthy one. We must allow ourselves to care about ourselves—to the proper limit and degree.

The purpose of this book is not to add to people's confusion about playing around with their minds—to cater to the wish for altered or higher consciousness. *The Inner Enemy* is about taking a more benign, tolerant interest in oneself, knowing and accepting oneself, being compassionate rather than critical toward oneself, even being interesting to oneself.

The quality of our self-interest is what is important, but most people's self-interest is skewed in one of two directions. People in the first group are inordinately self-concerned— without deriving any pleasure from it. They are forever dwelling on the inner soap opera, navel gazing, rehashing, analyzing. They are always questioning: Who am I? Why do I do things this way? Why did I say that? Why can't I do this? What's wrong with me? They wallow in hopeless, self-denigrating, accusatory moods. All that attention to themselves, and they never have any fun. For when they persist in asking such self-critical questions, the twerp is only too happy to provide the answers in gory detail, and those answers aren't what they want to hear.

Dwelling on one's failings and weaknesses and imperfections, striving always to be more loving, more understanding—as so many people do so guiltily these days—are in themselves indications of a powerful, critical, primitive Inner Enemy.

Then there is the hedonist's version of self-interest. Look at how many of the seemingly self-indulgent things people do are really self-defeating. They go out to parties every night, drinking, eating, dancing—and feel terrible, tired, hung over, and guilty all the next day. They coddle themselves, they think, by staying in bed an extra ten minutes each morning—and lose their jobs. They treat themselves to wonderful new clothes and then agonize over the bills. They sleep with a different partner each night and wonder why the thrill is gone. In this light, self-indulgent behavior makes the life of an ascetic seem more satisfying and pleasurable.

What then composes proper, healthy self-interest?

Balance is a vital ingredient. Balance both in *quantity*—in the allocation of self- and other-concern—and in *quality*—the tenor and direction of one's self-interest. It's a management skill, a matter of finding the right position on the broad spectrum running from self-indulgence to neglect.

Many psychological studies in the field of prosocial behavior have established that self-concern and knowledge are prerequisites for other-concern and knowledge. People with self-respect respect others. People who take care of themselves are more likely—and more able—to care for others. Self-criticism and self-denying behavior eventually render us too weak and distracted to have energy for others. Too much self-involvement blinds us to others' needs.

It's also important that self-concern have a proper focus.

Too many people spend time on brooding, negative intro-
spection, wondering what's wrong with them, listening in to
their garbled, ranting inner voices. They rarely hear supportive voices, don't give themselves much credit for the good
things they do, the clever things they think, their honorable
and caring behavior. There is no balance of positive and negative voices, no search for inner allies and self-support. Another way in which people misdirect their self-concern is by
doing things that outwardly seem self-caring or indulgent but
are, in fact, self-destructive: drinking, smoking, overeating,
taking drugs, partying all night, sleeping half the day, taking
from friends and family without any return. Then there are
others who are so full of themselves, so apparently confident
and unintrospective, so hidden behind a screen of activity,
that they barrel through life like a Mack truck, running down
everything in the way—their friends and loved ones as well
as their true selves. The reckless daredevil who challenges
the impossible, the blowhard who alienates friends with
bombastic speeches, the success-driven businessman are not
free of the twerp, merely ignorant of its presence.

Another of the many pitfalls along the way to self-knowl-
edge and healthy self-interest is the inability of many people
to accept the diverse, overlapping, multifaceted nature of
their thinking. They are uncomfortable with their seemingly
conflicting desires, statements, actions, and dreams. They
keep trying to pin themselves down. They want facts about
themselves; they dislike contradictions. They are much more
comfortable if they can find a pattern for their behavior, if
they can put a label on it: "I'm stingy." "I'm jealous." "I'm
neat." "I'm compulsive about food."

The desire for simplicity and clarity is understandable.
The number and diversity and seeming contradictions of the
human thought process seem unnatural and confusing. People feel tense and anxious about the baffling workings of their

minds; they seem abnormal, even crazy. They are sure no one else has such weird, deranged thoughts. No one else is so full of fears, or does such crazy, irrational, destructive things. So, in order to stop the inner turmoil, to gain peace of mind, they fall back on simple labels. They simplify their lives so fewer choices have to be made. They stay where they are, where they know the territory. They make dangerous, untrue generalizations about themselves so they don't have to evaluate each new action. They would rather label themselves "I'm jealous" than have to come to terms with the many different degrees and contexts in which their jealousy varies, to have to reevaluate the situation each time. In exchange for the seeming comfort of a label, they judge themselves; eventually they believe in the judgment and feel even more threatened and anxious when a new thought or situation challenges that label. To quote Gilbert and Sullivan, "A most amusing paradox."

"Single-mindedness" is a myth; it is not some ideal goal of mental health. In trying to force every thought and emotion into a knowable, fixed pattern, in the desire for simple answers and peace of mind, people betray their true natures. The complex tangle of multiple thoughts and voices which seems so baffling and causes such anxiety is natural—that is the way the human animal thinks.

> In the study of ideas, it is necessary to remember that insistence on hard-headed clarity issues from sentimental feeling, as it were a mist, cloaking the perplexities of fact. Insistence on clarity at all costs is based on sheer superstition as to the mode in which human intelligence functions. Our reasonings grasp at straws for premises and float on gossamers for deductions.[1]

1. A. N. Whitehead, "Adventures in Ideas," in Marshall McLuhan and Quentin Fiore, *The Medium Is the Massage—An Inventory of Effects* (New York: Bantam Books, 1967), p. 10.

It is undoubtedly nerve-racking to contend with such a barrage of input, and it would certainly be easier if all the messages came through loud and clear from one central source, but people exacerbate the tension by trying to make things fit a pattern and by feeling that they're crazy or neurotic when they can't.

Another major stumbling block to knowing and accepting oneself is the power of the image in our society. It is very hard to be yourself when there is constant pressure—overt or subtle—to live up to an image dictated by social and economic stereotypes. Images are pervasive in this country. People are saturated with messages everywhere they turn—on TV and radio, in movie magazines and newspapers, on billboards. They are handed down from parents, teachers, church, and community. Whether people think they're susceptible or not, these images have their effect.

It's very hard not to fall for imaged ideas of what's acceptable, of what others love and are attracted to, of what constitutes success. There's tremendous pressure in our culture to be special, to be celebrated, and it leaves many people feeling inadequate. They feel like failures if they don't measure up in beauty, talent, intelligence, or wealth to those images they are told are necessary for their well-being. People find it hard to accept themselves as they are, with their unique attributes, their own achievements and failings.

It is all too easy to get caught up in image making, in presenting to the world the composite of ingredients we feel will make us most acceptable. But this kind of imaging is dangerous and self-defeating, for in so doing we become alienated from our very core. We give up our true selves for safety and security, for relief from anxiety. The price of conformity is high, because if we drift far enough away from our true selves, if we give up too much, if we grow to disdain those qualities that are unique to us, we lose ourselves completely.

We have no one to come home to, only the security-seeking, approval-seeking Inner Enemy.

Image making is perhaps most dangerous when we are unlucky enough to succeed at it. Success at conforming to parental and societal expectations can be insidious. There are many people who seem to have it all—career, family, friends, recognition—who live up to every expectation of the good life. They come to therapy seeking help: They cannot understand why they are so depressed, why they feel like impostors, why they feel unfulfilled. What often happens is that the person has become successful at something that means little to him, is living a life that doesn't feel right. Sometimes he can't even remember what it was he wanted, who he was before. He has betrayed himself for the love and safety of acceptance. It has been Dr. Bach's experience in his many years of treating Hollywood celebrities that the more recognized and revered by the public a person is, the larger the gap between his public image and his private self, the more active and unrelenting the Inner Enemy. It is the widely recognized, highly imaged celebrities who have the most powerful Inner Enemies! Not one of Dr. Bach's famous patients did not at some point in his career, when self-doubts and his feelings of being an impostor, of deceiving his public, were running rampant, have thoughts of suicide. Gaining access to the Inner Dialogue is crucial to healthy self-concern. For if we are to be successful—i.e., if we are to be true to ourselves and grow—the security-conscious, image-worshipping Inner Enemy must be dealt with.

"I am a lucky woman. Two years ago we—my husband and three sons and I—were living in Darien, Connecticut. It's a typical upper-middle-class commuter suburb. I had, I thought, everything I wanted—a beautiful and impressive home, cars, clothes. I was active in the kids' schools, in the community. Everyone thought of me as the perfect wife and mother. I was considered a community leader; a couple of my programs won awards. The kids were doing fine. My husband was always overworked, but he was loving and kind. But I was miserable, always a bit depressed. I never felt quite satisfied. And that made me feel more depressed, and guilty, because I didn't know why. When I finally went into therapy, it came out pretty quickly that as nice as my life was, it wasn't my life. It was a shock to me. I'd managed to keep so busy that I never stopped to consider that I'd given up many old goals and dreams, that there were interests and talents I'd all but forgotten. Just realizing the cause of my depression was a tremendous relief. Change has come slowly—I was pretty radically off course—but now I've given up almost all the committees and just do a few things in connection with the boys. I'm completely involved in my studies and research on American folk art. I go to shows and museums, traipse around the country looking for artists. I no longer spend hours at the club, wasting time. My husband has been very supportive. And inspired, too. He's starting to make some changes that are important to him."

Awareness of, and fairness to, oneself are the primary aspects of sane self-concern. We must resist the temptation to image ourselves and be willing to tune in to and heed who we really are. By subsisting on images, by trying to simplify our inner lives, we impoverish ourselves. In the end we need to come home to ourselves—and without inner friends, we can be very lonely indeed. However surrounded by family and community, we need inner allies to offset terrorization by the Inner Enemy. We must find our self-respect within, for no amount of society's approval—of our image—will make up for our own judgment of our worth. Difficult as it is to be self-verifying in the face of outside pressure, we must find, through exploring the Inner Dialogue, the courage to pursue our inner voices and needs, to be interesting to ourselves. (See Part II: Stalking the Inner Enemy.)

And we must extend compassion and understanding to

ourselves, allow room to make mistakes and to grow without fear of harsh judgment or punishment. We must take ourselves off the hook of impossible or misdirected expectations, let go of unrealistic goals that turn us against ourselves when we fail. We must show the Inner Enemy that we are onto its game, that we are ready to give it its due if it will play fair.

4

Where Does the Inner Enemy Come From?

VOLUMES OF PSYCHIATRIC research attest to the existence of the Inner Enemy and to the often self-defeating nature of human endeavor. Understanding this phenomenon has been the subject of study for as long as there have been psychologists, psychiatrists, and sociologists, because the Inner Enemy is the number one enemy of mental health. Also, many patients in analysis or therapy have spent the lion's share of their treatment time wondering *why* they were so self-defeating, what in their background or character predisposed them to such anxiety and unhappiness.

To a point it is useful to understand the origins of our behavior, to identify precipitating factors, for often just the insight into the source of our present-day problem is enough to bring relief and even change. But it is possible to spend too much time delving deeper and deeper to seek the *why* of our self-inhibiting behavior without any constructive attempt at change in the present. The continued use of childhood traumas can be counterproductive in adulthood. The dwelling on and reliving of those traumas all too easily can become part of the self-destructive mechanism we use to exacerbate and prolong the influence of the Inner Enemy. The material becomes entrenched, the voice of the Inner Enemy amplified. Dwelling on the *why* becomes another way to avoid taking action. In the hands of an unethical or ineffectual therapist, the repeated reminder of and search for the childhood origins of the present-day Inner Enemy can keep the patient pinned fearfully to the couch.

Many people are inhibited and fearful of the quest into the mysteries of the mind. This fear is abetted by the psychological terminology with which the subject is discussed and by the aura of authority surrounding the psychiatric community. It is interesting to note that such labels as id, ego, superego, cathexis, and parapraxis were not coined by Freud, but that these off-putting Latin and Greek terms came about in the American translations of Freud's work. Bruno Bettelheim points out[2] that Freud went out of his way in his writings to demystify, dejargonize, and personalize his findings so that even lay people might easily understand and identify with them. Further, Freud did not feel that one need be a doctor in order to practice psychiatry, or that its training and practice should be so rigidly circumscribed.

This chapter touches briefly on some theories and reasons—the authors' and others'—for the existence and power of the Inner Enemy. But beyond a point it is less important to understand why we have an Inner Enemy and where it comes from than to examine the nature of the beast, to take it off its pedestal and figure out what to do about it in our personal lives.

Everyone has an Inner Enemy in some shape or form. No one completely escapes its clutches. The Inner Enemy is part of the human condition, part of our psychic heritage. We are all born small, helpless, inadequate creatures into a huge, un-

2. Bruno Bettelheim, "Reflections: Freud and the Soul," *The New Yorker*, March 1, 1982.

manageable world. We are literally babes in the wilderness. We cope with this frightening situation by accepting the verdict of the cold, cruel world, joining in the belief that we are weak, dependent, and compliant in order to placate powerful forces. The Inner Enemy is nature's way—human nature's way—of coping with the situation.

The Inner Enemy is an earthy creature. It identifies with our most basic instincts. It's interested in eating, sleeping, and fornicating, and hasn't much use for the complex, fancy lives we try to lead, or for the distance we seem to put between our basic emotions and needs and those fancy lives. In a way, the Inner Enemy is a sociogenetic monitor of evolutionary tendency. As the world changes faster and faster and loses its sense of human scale, as it distances us from our inner selves, the Inner Enemy acts as a brake on the too speedy evolutionary accelerator. It reminds us of where we come from. "Who do you think you are?" it asks. "You still fart and screw and secretly like peanut-butter sandwiches. Take it easy. Don't forget. Don't lose yourself." It is a voice cautioning us not to venture unprepared too far afield on our own. The Inner Enemy is like a throwback, a vestigial tail we no longer need now that we have conquered the elements and are in fact no longer at the mercy of fire, thunder, and wild animals. But though the Inner Enemy tends to be a bully and a hindrance to our growth, there are positive aspects to its reminders not to be fooled by the trappings of civilization, by our three-piece suits and televised images. The twerp always sees us with our clothes off—and sometimes we forget to look often enough.

The Inner Enemy fills a needed if misdirected role as a superficially safe and unthreatening (but ultimately self-destructive and hampering) channel for fear, anger, and guilt. Subtle and complex, it is a product of convoluted thinking. The Inner Enemy's *modus operandi* is that in sabotaging ourselves, we beat others to the punch. We hurt ourselves before others can hurt us. We exorcise our fear that we will turn our aggression against others, and thus forfeit their love and their good opinion of us. In turning against ourselves, we assuage our guilt about our dreams and successes, guilt about our anger that we weren't loved for ourselves. We do penance for going against our parents—for being different from what they had wanted, for betraying their expectations, for accomplishing what we were told we could never do. We prove—by falling short of our goals—what we have always feared about ourselves: *They were right.* And in doing so, we find comfort and relief—if temporary. We keep ourselves in check so as not to anger or threaten our loved ones, the gods, society at large. By bringing punishment on ourselves, we hold off the possibility of outside sources administering the punishment. We cut the odds on the chance of something really terrible happening—a dread disease, being struck by lightning, losing a beloved.

Everyone has an Inner Enemy, but everyone's Inner Enemy is different. The twerp is more prominent and powerful in some people than in others. The arenas in which it is active in each person's life differ. One person, for example, never doubts that his friends and family love him, but he worries himself sick about his health, seeing every little headache or pimple as a harbinger of death. Another never trusts the genuineness of the affection and concern shown by his wife, but has never doubted for one minute his ability to do his job well, or that he will live to be a hundred. Another person's Inner Enemy never stops badgering him about his weight and his less-than-perfect complexion, but the voices of dread and innuendo are silent when he steps out on the tennis court. Still another seems to come down with the flu, or a headache, or a pulled muscle every time she successfully completes a work project.

The fact is that we may all be born babes in the wilderness, with an Inner Enemy only too willing to exploit our weak position, but whether it takes hold, and to what degree and in what areas of our lives, has to do with what happens next. For as we grow, the Inner Enemy changes—expanding, diminishing, shifting focus—in accordance with our needs, depending on how our sense of personal power and impact grows and develops. If a child is given the feeling that he is acceptable as he is, that he is acknowledged for his unique qualities, that his words and actions have effect, his Inner Enemy will never gain a strong foothold.

Unfortunately, this is rarely the case. Even the most well-meaning parents will be blind at times to their children's individuality in favor of doing what they feel is the "right thing" for them. Their expectations for their children are formed by societal norms; they want them to be happy, to have the best, not to be ostracized. They themselves were treated the same way. They don't remember their own dreams; they've forgotten who they were. They perpetuate the same cycle in their children, wanting them to adjust, to fit in successfully to the only kind of life they believe can be rewarding. They pass on images of fulfillment that are the only ones they know. They praise the wrong thing—conformity—and punish or deride deviation. Sadly, this is not their intention.

The ways in which a child apprehends the information that he must change to be loved and accepted are subtle and indirect. He is praised for going along with what is expected of him, for "behaving," and he is chided for liking or enjoying things his parents feel are wrong or unproductive. He is denied chances to make simple choices—even in food and clothing or books. He is scolded for voicing an unacceptable opinion or for demanding explanations of what seem to him parental whims.

Anna Freud talked about the child *introjecting*—i.e., internalizing, or taking to heart—the attitudes of the critical parent. Against the stronger parent (or teacher or community), a child's opinion or belief about himself, about his own desires and attributes, cannot prevail. The child knows that powerful people—his parents—can make or break him, and he must assume that they are wiser than he. The child comes to believe in his parents' advice and judgment. He is in a no-win situation. The attitude he adopts is: "If you can't beat 'em, join 'em." He readjusts his thinking to conform to this new theory: "Father thinks there's something wrong that I don't like sports. And Father loves me. And he is grown up, so his opinion of me must be right." The child gives his parent the benefit of the doubt in order to maintain the illusion that he is loved, in order not to face his anger at not being seen for who he really is. He cannot win the fight for a fair opinion and treatment of himself, so in order to be able to live with himself and his father, he accepts his father's opinion. He turns the judgment on himself: "There must be something wrong with me."

He colludes with his father in order to believe in his father's love yet feels guilty at his anger that he cannot be loved for himself. Eventually this critical voice becomes internalized and independent, and his father's judgment becomes his own: "There *is* something wrong with me." The introjection will develop very specific components, dependent on the focus and degree to which his individuality and love were denied. "It is wrong of me to get angry." "It is wrong of me not to like baseball." "It is wrong that I'm not beautiful." This transfer of judgment to the self seems the only way to cope, the only way to preserve the image that one is loved. Powerless to strike back, guilty that he wishes to do so, the child turns the aggression against himself.

Dr. Alice Miller[3] expresses this idea a bit differently. Her thesis is that children, especially gifted or sensitive ones, give up their true needs and feelings in order to be the way their

3. Alice Miller, *Prisoners of Childhood* (New York: Basic Books, 1981).

parents want them to be and thus hold the love they feel they would otherwise lose. Moreover, in doing so they must create and believe in the illusion that their parents were good and their childhoods happy. They do this so well and successfully that they carry this fiction all through their lives, and thus suppress their true natures and their feelings about what they gave up. They cannot understand why they feel lonely and depressed, angry and alienated. Often outwardly successful as adults, their emotions are always under control and their real feelings a mystery to them. They don't *know* or remember their true selves, because as children they were never allowed to show their real feelings, to explore their own quirks and fancies. It was too risky to the parental relationship. The perpetuation of the fantasy of the happy childhood and the continued denial of true feelings is necessary: It would be too painful and enraging to acknowledge the loss of self, and to acknowledge that their parents did not love them as they really were. Also, over the course of time, the child—and then the adult—becomes as critical as the parent of those things about himself which were found wanting.

The power of each person's Inner Enemy, then, has to do first with how strongly and deeply outside parties—especially the parents—found fault with or refused to recognize the child's true nature; and second, with how easily and for how long the child acquiesced in that opinion.

Fear of the loss of love is the force behind the installation of the Inner Enemy. Theoretically, therefore, the meaner and the more critical and recognition-denying the parent, the stronger the introjection—the Inner Enemy. There is a paradoxical element to this, however. It is also true that the child of difficult, critical parents will recognize the situation and rebel against the tyranny of their opinion at an earlier age than the child of "nice" parents who are nonetheless guilty of not seeing the child's true self. Seduced by their apparent love for him, the child of "nice" parents has a hard time seeing what is wrong with his situation and feels guilty about his hostility.

When a child can differentiate his own from his parents' opinion, when he can say, "No, that's not me," or "No, I don't go along with that conclusion," then he is confronting the Inner Enemy and diminishing its power. The child slowly ejects the introjection by differentiating himself from his parents, by not colluding in their opinion, by being strong enough not to accommodate their wishes for him.

In treating patients, Dr. Bach always asks them to remember the crucial time in their lives when they first said, "No, they are wrong," or "They don't understand me," or "I think it's all right for me to be this way." Only when the child can have his own opinion of himself can he feel any sympathy for the parent's misunderstanding. Until then, he can only hate the unloving parent—i.e., the mother or father who loves the image or idea of the child rather than the real thing—and then turn the hate against himself out of guilt and powerlessness.

Safe as it may seem at the time, the price for knuckling under to the demands and opinions of the twerp can be devastating: It is no less than giving up ourselves in exchange for the appearance of love and acceptance, for not having to confront guilt, anger, and fear. As long as the Inner Enemy can be channeled in well-worn, manageable paths, we can keep the lid on our unconscious. We don't have to open that fearsome baggage we carry around. We don't have to face the threat of being devastated to learn that the selves we've learned to call our own are not our real selves at all. We needn't recognize that there are warring factions within our minds, which if let loose might tear us asunder. Change—confronting the Inner Enemy—is terrifying with so much at stake. It is understandable that our failures comfort us and our successes threaten us. Self-defeat solaces.

Knowing something about how the Inner Enemy works,

accepting that to some extent it is just part of human nature, gives us a new outlook on *insecurity*. We chastise ourselves for having foolish fears and doubts and lapses in self-esteem. We are continually anxious about our anxieties. Looking at the twerp this way, it does not seem so much of an aberration, a neurotic or fantasized demon. It is normal, real, a coping mechanism that allows us to live with ourselves in the face of conflicting opinions, alien forces, thwarted love, unfocused hostility. The achievement of adulthood from childhood can be measured as a degree of *emergence* from the influence of the Inner Enemy's power. The twerp, allied with the regressive influences, does all it can to slow down that emergence. In facing up to the Inner Enemy, we confront the forces that alienate us from our true selves. We turn the anger, the thwarted expectations of love, and our guilt for wanting to fulfill ourselves into the kind of energy which makes that fulfillment possible.

5

The Potential for Change Aggression: For or Against the Self?

So HOW CAN YOU fight the Inner Enemy? It cannot be ignored, for it is unavoidably present and will become more active and vociferous if it is not acknowledged. Denying its existence only provokes it to more violent outbursts. Trying to escape it also leads to trouble—for isn't that the objective of alcoholics, drug addicts, even of people who spend all night in deafening discos or immerse themselves in their work to the exclusion of all else?

Though it is not possible—or even desirable—to silence the Inner Enemy, it is possible to subdue it, to show it we're not intimidated by its overbearing tactics. By accepting the existence of the Inner Enemy, even befriending it, we turn the tables on it and take more control over the management of our inner voices.

Managing the twerp is an ongoing battle between the forces of success and failure, of self-realization and self-defeat, of pro-life and anti-life forces, of constructive and destructive aggression, of contracting or expanding horizons. Constant watchfulness is necessary if we are to move forward, because the twerp is an opportunist and will rush to enter wherever there is a vacuum, a doubt, any indecision.

This complicates ferreting out the Inner Enemy, for sticking up for oneself is just the sort of thing that gets it riled. Fearing success as it does, the twerp will do everything in its power to stop it. It is when we start moving ahead, learning and growing, that the twerp becomes active. It is when we *decide* to be successful, when we move in the direction of self-respect, that we must be most watchful for the twerp's vengeance.

The Inner Enemy's reactions to our attempts to change can be scary enough to make us give up. When this happens it is good to remember that in many ways the twerp is just a troublesome overgrown brat, too big for its britches, and that one of the reasons it has had such power is that it has convinced us it would make mincemeat of us if we stepped out of line. Just like the class bully, much of what it says is bluff, and it's time to stand up to it. The Inner Enemy is the single most important obstacle between where we are and where we want to be—not time, or money, or outer enemies.

While the twerp remains underground, shrouded in mystery, it can be fearsome indeed. Once we blow its cover, become aware of how it operates, spot and label its behavior, we considerably deflate its terrorist image. This consciousness-raising component of dealing with it is important, for the more we know and understand the Inner Enemy, the less intimidating and mysterious it is and the more prepared we are to develop tactics to cope with it. As we track down this elusive prey, adding fact after fact, observation after observation, to its dossier, as we become more familiar with its ways, the Inner Enemy loses its sting. "Oh, here it comes again," we can say, "I know this ruse." Forewarned, we brace ourselves for its attack. We muster our allies to defend ourselves. It is only if we ignore it or fail to give it its due that it will run amok.

KEEPING GOALS IN PERSPECTIVE

It is important to remember that there are limits to the change we can expect, and that we should not set impossible goals for ourselves when dealing with the Inner Enemy. We are looking for a realignment of the power structure, not an obliteration of those forces that seem to be against us. We are looking to rechannel our aggressions and anxieties, not eliminate them.

Because people manage their anxieties and anger so poorly, so troublesome and debilitating are they, they become *really* tense trying to get rid of them. People sometimes get the idea that the object of mental health is some kind of blissful, anxiety-free state in which one doesn't feel any anger or aggression. This is a big mistake—and in itself is an example of the Inner Enemy setting you up for a fall.

The truth is that anxieties are natural: They are what drive us, in whatever direction, for better or for worse. Some people manage their anxieties well. They use them to fuel their hard work, to spur their accomplishments, to make a desired impact on others and on the world. Their aggressive impulses earn them attention and respect and get them where they want to be.

But most people's anxieties hold them back, distract them, keep them always off-balance and ill at ease. They circle like vultures looking for vulnerable spots. They cause worry and panic, and they don't go away. When anxieties become entrenched, spontaneity goes out the window; behavior becomes rigid and limited to conform to the demands of inner demons.

"The fact that I'm afraid to fly rules my life. Years ago I broke up with a man I liked very much because he loved to travel, and I couldn't overcome my fears. For a long time I made up excuses, because it embarrassed me, and finally I broke up with him rather than have to admit my problem or do something about it. I've had several chances to take vacations with friends which I've had to pass up. I try and make a joke of it, but I worry about the issue coming up all the time. And it makes me feel very bad about myself."

"To me, my sex life with my husband is not very satisfying—and it's really my fault. Every time I try to tell my husband what pleases me, or to discuss sex, I clam up. I've got it all built up in my head that he'll think I'm strange and he'll be very angry, or he'll feel I'm blaming him. Meanwhile, I find it hard to enjoy our lovemaking, but nothing will change unless I do something about it."

"I've become so terrified of not getting an erection when I make love that I hardly ever pursue any potential relationship to the point where we would sleep together. I find myself terrified that my date will make advances. Yet I have no trouble with erections when I'm alone."

We need our anxieties to fuel our creativity, to bring about growth and change. Without them, we would stagnate. What we need to do is redirect them to our service and away from inhibiting our growth. A neurotic person is one whose ego is weakened by internal enemies; a healthy person can manage them. Paradoxically, the way to cope with the Inner Enemy is by opening up rather than clamping down on it. When it is out in the open, we can learn how the Inner Enemy operates and then learn the skills and tactics to deal fairly with it.

Man is a problem solver by nature. By seeking solutions, forging trails, making choices, he grows and moves forward. Stalking the Inner Enemy can be a particularly satisfying challenge because in it there is tremendous potential for self-help and management. And the resulting self-control and confidence are the very things that put the Inner Enemy in its place.

TAKE A STAND FOR THE SELF

So, where do we begin to do battle with the Inner Enemy? The first step is to declare our intent to stand up and fight. The declaration itself is therapeutic, for the Inner Enemy loves indecision. We throw down the gauntlet to those demons who want to keep us in check, who want to see us fearful and failing. We make a decision to go easy on ourselves, to act in our own best interest, and to move forward in directions of our own choosing. We declare that we are no longer willing to go along with the opinions and actions of inner voices that will not show themselves and have decided to keep us down. We make a decision to do what we can to learn about our Inner Enemy and to learn the skills and tactics necessary to fight back.

GIVE THE DEVIL HIS DUE

If we recognize the right of the Inner Enemy to exist and we acknowledge its power, we are in a better position to fight back. The Inner Enemy loves it when people pretend it's not there or of no account. Then it can go about its business, messing up their lives, and they don't even realize what's happening.

It needs room to breathe, and it needs reassurance that you are aware of its existence. Once it realizes that you know what's going on, it will think twice before doing something foolish. And if you let it know you accept it and are willing to work with it and that its existence isn't in danger, it will even let up on you. The Inner Enemy is oversensitive and vindictive, but you can appeal to its sense of fairness and make it play your way. Also, by letting it have its way sometimes and learning that even then you can cope with it, you gain a perspective on your own strength.

ACCESS TO THE INNER DIALOGUE

The balance of this book is about how to get to know the Inner Enemy and what to do about it. The way we do that is slowly, in small steps, in a controlled and safe way, take the lid off the unconscious. We learn to relax our desperate clutch on all its fearsome secrets and bring them to the light. We encourage debate among the inner voices in an atmosphere of fairness and good will. The many tactics and techniques by which we accomplish this, which are explained in detail in Parts II and III, are outlined briefly here.

The first step in managing the Inner Enemy is to listen in and find out who's talking in there. By tuning into the Inner Dialogue, monitoring what goes on, we familiarize ourselves with the various voices and learn what they have to say. We learn who's for and who's against us. We become aware of the power structure just by paying attention to when certain voices chime in and when they're quiet. We find out what provokes them. We get an idea about what form of government seems to be operating—is it a dictatorship? A democracy? Are parliamentary procedures followed, or do all the voices shout one another down to get attention? Which voices have the most power? Are certain voices easily subdued or pushed aside? We come to know the circumstances under which certain voices and behaviors surface.

As we come to understand the workings of our inner voices, we become more able to impose some order on them. We get to the point where we can actively encourage debate, and gain confidence in our ability to let the voices have their say without being overwhelmed by them. Our self-consultations become healthier, more balanced. We lessen the risk of having negative voices overly influence our decisions. The voices that seemed so elusive become more friendly and understandable and predictable; we no longer feel at their mercy. A logic or pattern about how we think and feel about ourselves takes shape. We can adopt a more fluid attitude toward our conflicting and seemingly paradoxical voices and allow that they all have a place in the scheme of things. It is no longer of such importance to make everything fit a theory or pattern.

Once we gain enough confidence in our ability to cope with the many conflicting voices and are able to allow them to have their say—even at the risk of negative or destructive commentary—we take the bite out of the Inner Enemy's power to hurt and surprise us.

In this process we look at the machinations of the Inner Dialogue in the present, we see how it affects our lives now. While understanding the Inner Enemy's origins in our childhood, we focus on our desire to know and be who we want to be now in spite of our past history.

As we become increasingly able to listen in to our voices, we find that there are positive voices, too, which haven't been given a fair hearing. We learn to single them out and cultivate their support, and get to the point where we can call upon them in our confrontations with the twerp. We can allocate more and more energy to our healthy growth-directed selves, less to the demands of our mean-spirited consciences. In this way we can short-circuit the harsh judgments of the Inner Enemy and give our allies a fair say, especially when it comes to administering rewards and punishments. Our loyal and supportive allies leaven the judgments of the suspicious, punitive twerp. By ferreting out those inner allies, befriending them, strengthening and arming them, we muster support for our conflicts with the Inner Enemy. We make it possible to have a fair contest.

MEANS OF ACCESS

There are numerous ways in which you learn to listen to the Inner Dialogue, and most of the tactics are very simple. The simplest is just to stop for a few minutes from time to time to see if you can catch your thoughts. Elusive and complex and fast moving as these thoughts are, with a bit of practice you can learn to sort some of them out. There are guided-imagery techniques in which you allow your mind to wander in a planned, controlled way. Dreams are another important means of access that can be explored without a degree in psychology. Later in the book, tactics for keeping journals, monitoring dialogues, and holding debates with the Inner Enemy are discussed. There are exercises to help you use and make sense out of daydreaming techniques for self-consultation, and exercises to encourage you to share the Inner Dialogue with others in your life.

WHAT IS THE PAYOFF?

Obviously an organization in which the voices of the Inner Enemy have the upper hand is a poorly managed one. In order to reorganize the power structure, we have to rally support from every possible ally and build the skills to keep everything running smoothly. We develop a first-strike capacity that puts the Inner Enemy on the defensive for a change. In substituting healthy new patterns for creaky old habits, we turn around that aggression which is now undermining our hopes and dreams. We see that anxieties and aggression can be powerful forces for our growth and well-being. We reduce our susceptibility to being terrorized by ghosts whose messages are incongruous with the true facts and circumstances of our lives.

The rewards of taking on the Inner Enemy can be tremendous, for as long as it is in control, we're not giving ourselves a fighting chance to be who we want to be and dream of being, of doing what we want to do. It is in the twerp's best interest to terrify us and discourage us from the quest, to tell us that things are perfectly OK as they are. And because we have learned to live with the twerp, because change seems so fraught with risk and the possibility of more failure and more anxiety, we often choose to play it safe and maintain the status quo. But this safety is a fraud, for once we start examining the Inner Enemy more closely, we see how incredibly defeating it is to be at the mercy of its demands. The price paid for bowing to those demands can be too much to bear, can bring us to ruin.

And to this tragedy is added the irony of what a paper tiger the Inner Enemy really is. If we can muster the strength to stand up to it and recognize the unfairness in giving it such power, we are already admitting that we are willing to fight for our self-respect and our success. In learning to fight fair with ourselves, we acquire one of the real keys to the maximization of our own potential, to the finding and appreciation of our lost selves, and to the establishment of sound relationships with others.

II
STALKING THE INNER ENEMY

6

The Nature of the Beast

So, what is this creep like? What does it say and do? How do we recognize it at work? What are some of the things that all our Inner Enemies have in common?

THE INNER ENEMY IS OLD HAT

Honed and refined by personal experiences, the Inner Enemy reflects our past ways of coping with contradiction and adversity. It changes its colors as experiences mold and reinforce it. Sometimes it becomes so entrenched, its reaction so imprinted, especially during important formative stages in our lives, that it doesn't keep up with the times. It's like an ex-self—it reminds us of someone we *used* to be, of a way we *used* to behave, yet we cannot seem to shake it. The twerp is a bad habit we no longer need. Like a dinosaur, it should have been extinct long ago, but it hangs on tenaciously and surfaces whenever it sees an opening.

This is why it is so often a mystery to us. The carping, critical twerp inside us seems incongruous with the outer reality of our lives. We live well and successfully, our friends and loved ones think we're just terrific, yet here's this creep, flying in the face of the evidence. We feel we have long outgrown our childhood habits, long ago cast off the images we had of ourselves as kids, yet we still have the same knee-jerk reactions.

John feels he has come a long way from the shy, awkward kid who was afraid to speak up in class. No one thinks of him that way today—why, some people think he is downright overconfident, handsome, animated, articulate. However, though he may project an air of confidence, he is shaking inside. He feels like an impostor. A little voice keeps piping up: "You think they're fooled. But they'll find you out. You'd better be careful."

The Inner Enemy is hopelessly out of date, not at all hip to the real circumstances of John's present life. The truth is that John's years of experience have given him a good deal of assurance. But he still cannot shake the twerp's threats and innuendoes. And the more distance he puts between that primitive voice and his substantial accomplishments, the more vindictive, demanding, and irrational it becomes. At times John becomes so bedeviled by his inner voices that he withdraws from his public life because he knows that when he does, he is much less anxious. He gives in and the Inner Enemy lets up on him. What he really must do, if he wants to break down those barriers which are holding him back, is confront the Inner Enemy head-on.

THE INNER ENEMY IS SHIFTY

It is not a monolithic, slow-moving target wearing a red coat, easy to get a good shot at. It is an accumulation of all the enemy voices, a walking encyclopedia of all the self-defeating, growth-impairing ways that worked so "successfully" in your past. It keeps a running inventory of your weaknesses. A wily, street-smart critter, it knows just what to pull out of its bag of tricks in any given instance. Anxiety attacks, fumbles, slips of the tongue, pratfalls, blunders—it has them for all occasions. The way it acts up when you are trying to sit quietly and read a book is very different from what it does when you are running around madly trying to get the kids off to school or when you are feeling sick.

And it can change at a moment's notice. Should you be successful in getting the Inner Enemy off your back about your weight, it will zero in on something new—your work habits, love life, athletic prowess, job security, lovability. At the very least it will dole out an incapacitating headache or a skinned knee.

The Inner Enemy likes to maintain a certain misery level, whatever it has to do to achieve it. It doesn't want things to go too easily for you, doesn't want you to have leftover energy to pull ahead. Have you ever noticed how your free-floating anxieties and self-criticism abate when a *real* problem comes up and things aren't going very well anyway? The Inner Enemy relaxes the pressure a little, figuring you have enough to keep you in line. It doesn't want you getting too big for your britches, and when you do, it will do everything in its power to bring you to heel.

THE INNER ENEMY WORKS UNDERCOVER

The twerp is not a fair fighter. Secretive and sneaky, it's the master of the surprise attack. The Inner Enemy can wreak havoc in our lives for years while we're in the dark about what's going on, for its ways are subtle, often seemingly unrelated to the problem we're able to identify.

For years Marion wanted to study ceramics at a nearby school, but she realized she was just too tired at the end of the day to have any energy for the class. It took her by surprise to realize she was tired *because* she wanted to take the class. The Inner Enemy was against it.

Whenever Brad had a good weekend with his kids, he would spend Sunday night in turmoil. He worried about whether they cared about him, whether anything bad would happen to them during the week. He was sure he had said or done the wrong things. Often he would drink Sunday night just to calm down. If he had had too good a time, he was sure to ruin it by calling his sons the next day and provoking an argument, or by having nothing planned for the next weekend. If things went badly the next weekend, he was upset but relieved.

Janet doesn't know why but whenever she meets a man she really likes, and wants to sleep with him, she comes down with a vaginal infection.

The Inner Enemy has many devious ways of keeping us off-balance. We may have dreams we can't remember that leave us feeling puzzled and uneasy. We may say or do things which are harmful and totally out of character. Our nonstop "thinking" may be so intense and confusing that it saps our energy. We may become ill without warning.

One way to spot the Inner Enemy's presence is to note when fair debate is threatened or interrupted. Note when your ruminations about a particular issue are suddenly usurped by a strident voice with all kinds of arguments—rational and otherwise—about why you shouldn't do it or try it: "It's too expensive." "I'm too old." "I won't have time." "It's foolish." "A waste of time." "I can't . . ." "I'll have to give up ——————." Suddenly, inexplicably, all the positive arguments are tossed aside in a floodtide of doubts and don'ts. The Inner Enemy often becomes especially active in times of crisis, of major decisions and life-changing debates, when the opportunity for growth is strongest.

Undetected, the Inner Enemy can do a great deal of damage. The best defense—the only defense—is to learn to recognize its tricks, to become aware of the specific ways it influences your life.

THE INNER ENEMY IS NEGATIVE

Joy is fleeting, but misery lingers on. The Inner Enemy is a tenacious creep, with a long memory. It can remember, and remind us, of every piece of bad news, every little failing, every fear. It helps us dwell on the minuses and trivialize the pluses, exaggerate failure and minimize success and accomplishment.

The Inner Enemy is a great museum builder. It keeps all the joyless, negative information on file and can display it at a moment's notice. It culls the collection for the worst, most frightening, most embarrassing tidbits. "Remember what a fool you made of yourself when you joined that volleyball game at the beach? That's almost as embarrassing as the time Emma turned you down for a date in front of Herb and Maria." "Why would you want to go white-water rafting? Don't you remember how terrified you were just on that little canoe trip last summer?" "You don't want to ask Ellen out. You'll be tongue-tied and uncomfortable." "Remember the time you took your son to play baseball in the park and struck out every time you were at bat?" The Inner Enemy searches out the Mona Lisa of the collection: "You made such an ass of yourself standing up in front of all those professors with your fly open. That beats all."

The Inner Enemy is a spoiler. It can be counted on to bring us down if we're having too much fun, being too carefree. Perhaps we're just enjoying a cup of coffee and staring out the window at the lovely spring day. The Inner Enemy will accuse us of wasting time, will start to list all the things that need doing in the garden, or will divert our thoughts to a friend who is ill.

Perhaps we're having lunch with friends we haven't seen in a while, having a wonderful time catching up, basking in their care for us. The Inner Enemy will remind us of the fight we had with Anne last year, will hark back to a friend who betrayed us twenty years ago, will look for clues in our friends' conversation that allow us to question the friendship.

The joylessness of the Inner Enemy is boundless. It loves worst-case scenarios: "What if I go to bed with Adam and he thinks I'm too skinny? What if he never calls again? Will he think I'm too promiscuous?"

"My wife and I took a week's vacation in Barbados, our first time away from the children in four years. We were both very excited about the trip—we'd planned it for months; my parents came to stay with the kids. Well, the minute we got there, Marie started worrying about the kids—and I mean every worry in the world: Were they sick? Had there been an accident? Were they eating right? Had she remembered to leave instructions about Kevin's medicine? Did my father know how to get to the hospital? Would the kids resent our going away? Would she ever forgive herself if something happened? Were they getting their sleep? Were they being allowed to watch too much television? At home, she's not much of a worrier. But here we had a rare chance to be alone, to enjoy ourselves, and she undermined the entire trip for both of us."

Self-critical, negative people end up spoiling not only their own enjoyment but that of others. They poison their surroundings with bad feelings. Usually they are negative and critical of others as well, as they spread ill feeling and doubt. They end up putting down everything: books, movies, causes, groups. Obviously, this contagious bad feeling has serious implications for parenting, friendships, and intimate relationships.

THE INNER ENEMY IS NARROWMINDED

A prominent characteristic of the twerp is its tunnel vision—it cannot deal with context. It tends to focus on simple traits, to make generalizations based on very few facts. This one-dimensional orientation is endemic to the Inner Enemy. It picks out little things that it notices about us and harps on them. It isolates behavior and is quick to draw conclusions, to stereotype and judge.

The Inner Enemy judges characteristics rather than contexts, and its frame of reference is outdated. It's like a parent who can see only that his son doesn't play baseball very well and ignores all the things he can do well: his popularity with his friends, his musical skills, his interest in animals, his wit, his good grades.

The world of complexity and paradox in which we live, the world of subtlety and nuance, makes the twerp uncomfortable. It can see only one thing at a time: "You have beady eyes," or "You didn't get an erection." In an atmosphere of fair debate, the criticism about our beady eyes is tempered by recognizing positive qualities about our looks: a generous mouth, good complexion, gracefulness, nice hair. And things other than our looks are factored in: character, temperament, talent, sense of humor. The twerp is blind to all this. In moments of fair debate, we recognize that the little voice challenging our ability to get an erection is against us, and we rally the voices that remember differently and question an erection as the be-all and end-all of sexual pleasure. Left unchecked, the twerp will go a step farther: "You have beady eyes" becomes "You're ugly." "You didn't get an erection" becomes "You're a lousy lover."

Another of the twerp's tactics is to find a "hook"—a past failure, a physical flaw, a weakness, a fear, an unhappy memory—and keep prodding and reminding and criticizing you about it until it grows way out of proportion. It becomes a barrier to progress, a way to keep you paralyzed. The less-than-perfect figure looms larger and larger as a barrier to falling in love. The job you were fired from twenty years ago becomes the reason for staying in a job you hate. The feeling of dread when you first sat behind the wheel of a car keeps you from learning to drive and drastically limits your horizons. The memory of wanting to flee from your family responsibilities becomes proof that you are a terrible mother. The Inner Enemy has no fresh material; it repeats the same tired things over and over. But it's an effective ploy, for when one negative, tyrannical lobbyist is able to shout down all other voices, you can become truly weakened, sick in mind and body.

The twerp loves simplifications, stereotypes, generalizations: "That was just like a typical female." "You're a real tightwad." "Your male chauvinism sure showed itself." It takes a fragment of behavior out of context and blows it up out of proportion. Of course, these seemingly innocent labels become self-fulfilling, more fuel for the fire of self-loathing.

THE INNER ENEMY IS RIGID

The twerp doesn't exactly go with the flow. It has fixed ideas about what's right and what's wrong, definite fascist tendencies. The Inner Enemy can intimidate us with its overbearing courtroom manner, its unrelenting criticism. It revels in blamesmanship—telling us what we did wrong, pointing an accusing finger at every minor infringement of its strict rules. It has outdated ideas about gender roles and doesn't like them to get mixed up. The Inner Enemy is always on the side of power—the parent, the cop, the teacher—which makes it hard for us to stand up to authority and fight for our individuality. It has taught us all too well that it will make trouble if we refuse to conform to the demands of others. In fact, we are rewarded with a false sense of well-being, a temporary slackening of anxiety, a tempting sense of approval, when we go along with the Inner Enemy. It loves us to get fixated on images of who we should be—for images are stereotyped, safe, inflexible.

THE INNER ENEMY IS A CHICKEN

As we grow older our impulse is to want to move forward in life, to learn and expand. The twerp wants us to stay home where it's comfortable. The battle is waged between our desire to achieve our goals and the forces of denial. All of our thinking processes reveal this struggle between the provocative, intensive process of evolving and developing ideas and the anti-creative, anti-intellectual forces that want us to remain rooted and stupid. The process of inner consultation, of wondering and brooding, is always tempered by voices of warning and caution, reductive judgments, criticism, dissuasions, and such comments as "What if . . . ?", "That's silly," "That will never work," "You can't do that," "They'll think you're a fool," "Be careful." Doesn't some of this sound like a parent--even a loving parent—reminding a child of his limitations, stressing safety, warning against venturing into new territory?

It is when we seek the truth about ourselves, when we learn to distinguish between our own dreams for ourselves and the dreams others have in mind for us, that the twerp becomes most vicious and active.

"For the last four years of my marriage, I knew there was no hope for it and wanted to end it. But every time I thought about leaving I would panic. I came up with literally hundreds of reasons why I would be a fool to leave, and most of them were negative: I'd be terrified living alone, I'd fall apart in any little emergency, the days would seem endless, all my friends would side with my husband, I'd miss the amenities of my life, I was too old to be a single woman again, no one would want me, it would be awful not to have anyone to talk to, I'd have to do much more housework since I couldn't afford help, I'd realize what a mistake I'd made and there'd be no turning back, I'd miss our trip to Arizona, Al was really a wonderful guy and I didn't appreciate him—and on and on. Every once in a while a little voice would try to get a word in edgewise: 'Are you kidding? You'll be much happier without Al. You used to love living alone. When have you ever been bored? Or without a date, for that matter? And where's your sense of adventure? And remember, there's no chance to get what you want here.' But those voices were rare and meek. All I could hear were the voices of caution and doom."

Our success is death to the Inner Enemy, because its power lies in our ignorance and the suppression of our dreams. When we go exploring, it will make us sick. When we try to create, it will visit us with overpowering fatigue. It will cause us to trip on the path, to give up in terror, to decide once again that the anxiety is too great, that we would rather be safe *and* sorry.

THE INNER ENEMY IS A DANGEROUS CREEP

7

Aha! Identifying Your Very Own Twerp's Behavior

WHAT ABOUT YOUR OWN Inner
Enemy? Can you find it? Are you aware of how it operates?
Do you know the areas and issues in your life that bring it
out? Do you know where and when you're safe from it?

This is the important part; for while broad generalizations are helpful, everyone's Inner Enemy is different in size
and shape, area of operation, tactics and behavior. And in
order to develop a plan for managing our own twerp better,
we have to pinpoint specific information about how it behaves and what it's up to. We have to break through its defenses and disguises and evasions, flush it out of the nooks and
crannies where it hides. An aggressive approach is needed if
we are to make a real breakthrough into the netherworld
where the twerp holds sway. We have been too easily intimidated, too easily sidetracked when we have tried to cope
with it.

Pinpointing the idiosyncrasies of our twerp serves two
purposes. First, we need this information if we are to evaluate its power and formulate a plan of action to bring it under
better control. Second, the very act of unmasking it takes

away some of its fearsomeness and ability to surprise and hurt us. It loses its mystery.

The more you can learn to label the behavior of your twerp and define its character, the more you rein in its ability to run rampant over your best interests. The more you can personalize it, develop a vocabulary to describe it, the more known its danger signals become; the more obvious its cues, the more you demystify it and upset its shadowy base of power. Prepared for its antics, you will have the wherewithal to abort its missions, defuse its bombs, and diffuse its impact. Every little bit of information you gather about the twerp blows its cover a bit more. You confiscate its weapons.

Uncovering your own Inner Enemy is quite a challenge; there's no question that it requires bravery and a willingness to take risks. But the risks are taken very slowly and safely, in an atmosphere of goodwill, in a spirit of curiosity and exploration. And it's not as though all the dark, raging torrent of the unconscious comes spewing forth at once. Knowledge and revelation about the Inner Enemy come in small increments—it is an ongoing process that builds personal strength as it goes, each step making you that much stronger and more able to take the next step. Also, in the process of uncovering the Inner Enemy, you discover ally voices to support the quest. The rewards for your success in uncovering your Inner Enemy are great: Not only do you break down some of the barriers you have put in the way of your own growth, but there is a great deal of richness, interest, and entertainment in learning about yourself—far more than you would think.

This and the following two chapters will help you flesh out the picture of your own Inner Enemy. There are examples, case histories, and questions to trigger your thoughts about the Inner Enemy's whereabouts and behavior. After you have gone through the material in these three chapters, you will have more information with which to fill out the Twerp Alert Report at the end of Chapter 9, in which you will itemize as specifically as possible the details of your twerp's behavior: When does it show up? What does it say? What conditions or situations in your life favor its activity? Be on the lookout for catchphrases it seems to respond to, redundancies, repetitions—any kind of material can go into your twerp dossier.

Answering these questions may not be easy. Your Inner Enemy is not likely to be open-handed and forthcoming with the information you want. After all, decades of carefully constructed defenses and deceptions are not going to fall away overnight just because you have declared war. In fact, the Inner Enemy may be more tenacious and afraid than ever when it realizes what you're up to. You must listen in without being intimidated by it.

TWERP AWARENESS

Are you having trouble seeing how the twerp operates in your life? Does it seem like the twerp is an interesting phenomenon, but it has nothing to do with you? If you're having a hard time seeing how the Inner Enemy relates to you, you may be one of those people lucky enough to have found ways to use their anxieties and aggressions constructively, to have found supportive voices in their Inner Parliament. But if you are anxious and feel your life is limited, without knowing why, chances are your Inner Enemy is acting up in ways you don't recognize—and about which it is happy to keep you in the dark. The Inner Enemy is lying low. You must look a little closer at the things that go wrong in your life and see if any of them are self-inflicted. Remember, the telltale mark of twerp behavior is that it is all under your control, not the responsibility of any outside person or situation.

The range and variety of twerp tricks are nothing short of amazing. Some are pretty obvious: It's the twerp who makes you overeat, makes you smoke too many cigarettes or drink too much—and then smothers you with guilt and remorse about it.

The twerp makes you forget things—your keys, your tennis date. More clever still, it merely makes you *worry* that you'll forget, so that you compulsively check for your keys or wallet every time you leave the house—even if you have *never* forgotten them. If you go out shopping to treat yourself to something and then feel guilty because you spent too much money, that's the twerp. If you drink at parties, even though you know it loosens your tongue and you say things you'll regret, or if you don't go to parties because you think no one will notice you, that's the twerp. If you don't want to bother the salesperson to show you another shirt, or feel you can't ask the bus driver to make an extra stop at your corner, that's the twerp. It's the twerp who makes you so clumsy some days that you can't cross a room without tripping or dropping something. When you can't stop blaming yourself for something that went wrong, when an incident best forgotten keeps replaying in your head, that's the twerp. It's the twerp who makes you say outrageous, provocative things and then presses others to go along with them: "I know you don't care about me, because if you did you would have come home in time for dinner." It's the twerp who makes you act cool and withdrawn with someone you love because of an imagined slight or transgression, and then use that distance as evidence that that person doesn't love you. When you doubt someone's love and attention and hold yourself in reserve, that's the twerp. When the person you've been keeping your distance from gets the message and pulls back, then the twerp celebrates—you may feel relieved, but you've lost another contest.

If something important or pleasurable never seems to get done, the twerp is probably getting in the way. If your talents and accomplishments never seem to live up to your expectations, maybe the twerp doesn't want you to feel good about them. If you own a big home and two cars and a swimming pool and belong to the best clubs and just got a promotion at the brokerage firm, and you gave up a promising career as a pianist or cabinetmaker to do so, maybe the twerp has steered you very far wrong. Perhaps you're an attractive woman who meets and dates many men, yet none of them seems to measure up to your dream of a mate or the dates never go anywhere: Maybe the twerp is doing its best to see that you don't find the sustaining relationship you say you crave.

Or you're a man who loves his wife, but you feel so terrified of caring so much for her that you have affairs—which both takes the pressure off your intense feeling for your wife and lets you run the risk of losing her if she finds out.

When you catch yourself in a moment of panic in the midst of a good time, or when amid exciting plans you're beset by doubts, the twerp is lurking.

Now is the twerp becoming more real?

Where Do I Find My Twerp?

Where do we look for clues to the Inner Enemy? To the Inner Dialogue, that incessant conversation we are engaged in. It contains all the information. All we need do is record the Inner Dialogue and the twerp is revealed.

Aye, there's the rub. Penetrating the complex and elusive Inner Dialogue is like solving Rubik's Cube blindfolded. It seems a simple matter of merely taking down what's being said in there until we pause to think about how fast those thoughts fly around and how confusing they are. After all, the only mandate of a patient in psychoanalysis is *to say what comes to mind as it comes to mind.* To free-associate and thereby uncover the twerp. However, anyone who has ever tried this, formally or informally, in and out of therapy, alone or with a friend, knows how elusive those inner voices are.

There are so many of them. They talk so fast, they contradict each other. They shout. They mumble. And something—a fearful, unrelenting dictator, an authority figure—seems determined to censure and fog up those messages. Dreams and daydreams evaporate in thin air. It is easy to become discouraged.

Little by little, however, we can pry open our reluctant unconscious and amplify those voices. And as we make progress, advancing in small steps, we gain confidence and ability for the next revelation and reassure ourselves that the dangers we had anticipated are only imagined. That in fact our new knowledge is liberating.

Chapter 10 is about techniques and tactics for getting closer to the Inner Enemy, exercises that will help you tune in to the Inner Dialogue. But go through these three chapters now, answer the questions whenever possible, let the examples and anecdotes trigger more questions and thoughts of your own. You will see which questions are hard to answer and what kinds of exercises might help fill the gaps.

NAME THAT TWERP

One of the first steps in establishing contact with your Inner Enemy is to give it a name, so you can address it directly, so you have a concrete way to think of it. In this book we refer to the Inner Enemy as the twerp, because that personifies how the authors think of him: an arrogant pipsqueak with false airs of power and importance, with nothing better to do than make trouble. To another the Inner Enemy is a monster, a creep, a jerk, a spoilsport, a cretin, a fool, an ogre, a deadbeat, a tyrant, a dictator.

Try to picture the Inner Enemy. Let your imagination go for a minute and see if you can visualize what it looks like. Is it a devil? A ghostly figure? A gnarled troll under a bridge? A fast-talking con man? A moustache-twirling silent-movie villain? A manipulative femme fatale? A beefy, pugnacious cop? Does it change according to the circumstances? How does it speak to you? In whispers? Outright insults? Threats of violence or failure? Syrupy-sweet talk? Constant harangues to work harder?

Have you called yourself any names today? Stupid? Dummy? Jerk? Asshole? Turkey? Have you been yelling at yourself, "What's the matter with me?" or "Why can't I do this faster?"

Think of some of the pranks the twerp has pulled lately. Has it made you late? Caused a fight with a friend? Encouraged a rash decision? Made you doubt someone's love?

Don't let the Inner Enemy be so elusive. Make it as real and graphic as possible. As you get to know it better, you will be able to add more detail to its description. But with whatever material you can gather now, label it in the way that best describes it for you. In a pinch you can even name it after a movie or TV character it reminds you of: Peter Lorre in *M*? The Joker in *Batman*? Darth Vader from *Star Wars*? The Wicked Witch of the West in *The Wizard of Oz*? If all else fails, just call it Joe. Or feel free to use the authors' name for the Inner Enemy: twerp.

WHAT SHOULD I DO NEXT?

For a couple of weeks, don't try anything more strenuous than reminding yourself to keep your antennae out, to tune in. Try to "capture" whatever comes your way, random thoughts, phrases, bits of conversations. Notice yourself daydreaming—and notice what you're daydreaming about. Make a conscious effort to tune in at various times, especially in likely situations: when you sit down to work, when you call your spouse or a friend, when you first look at yourself in the mirror in the morning, when you open the refrigerator. Two very important aspects of the Inner Dialogue to pay attention to: dreams, any little scrap; and actions, especially un-usual or accidental behavior, saying something by mistake, losing something, a mishap.

Encourage debate. Even if you can't pick up much of what's going on, allow the voices to babble on and ramble, with as little censoring as possible. This way the habit of al-lowing the voices to speak builds up. You let your inner self know you're ready to listen. You give the voices credibility. Further, set aside more time to daydream—even just to label the time as such. Tell yourself you're looking forward to dreaming at night and then remember to try and capture that dream—even a smidgen of it—the next morning. Make your-self an open forum for your voices, a place where all speakers are allowed.

Start right away to keep a journal, or some sort of note-book, to keep track of the twerp. This does not have to be elaborate. Just record whatever you can, in whatever form you can, as you find time—dreams, twerp cues, times and places of arrival, active periods, slogans, repeated arguments. The best way, of course, is to write down every detail you can capture of the Inner Dialogue as it happens. But even taking five minutes at the end of the day to write down your ex-periences with the twerp is a good start. Record even the seemingly insignificant fragments. All of this will help in compiling the Twerp Alert Report at the end of Chapter 9. Sample notations from the journals of students taking the Inner Enemy course:

Debate: "It's eleven now. The morning's gone. I can read these two magazines and have a bite and I'll start working on this chapter at noon."

"But you've already shuffled paper for an hour. If you'd do a little work—just an hour of work, even—you'd feel so relieved."

"I *will* work. If I start at twelve I can still put in five or six good hours."

"Why don't you work for just one hour now and then reward yourself with the magazines and a little lunch."

"But I don't know what to write. If I leaf through the magazines I can be thinking of what to write."

"You know that doesn't work. The longer you put it off, the worse you feel. That old feeling of dread is starting to come on. You can get rid of it simply by writing. Anything. It doesn't have to be perfect."

"Why should I write something just to write? It's a waste of time."

"It's not. It gets the juices flowing and gives you a place to start, something to work with."

Dream: The women in my business group came over for a meeting. I wasn't ready on time, couldn't find anything to wear. As women came in, they would wait in the living room very patiently. I was embarrassed that I hadn't even prepared coffee. A morning meeting. Door prizes. Two: One a binder with acetate pages—smaller, thinner than my photo albums; and a box which contains a selection of decorated glass candle holders. I didn't want them. Decided to award both door prizes. Discussion about this with one of the women. I tried to do something "artful" with the candles—red wax—a new use.

Daydream: Drawing out of doors, sultry air, but all conveniences of home—comfortable drawing table, many art supplies, no wind.

Called my parents today and dialed my boyfriend's number by mistake!

A voice, as I sat at my desk, saying: "If Alice really loved you, she would have made sure you remembered that appointment."

A voice: "Alice sure seems distracted when I get home from work."

A voice: "What do you suppose Alice is doing now?"

Dream fragment: A horse riding down a city street, away from me, in shadow, can't tell who's on horse.

Several times today I scolded myself for my "stupidity" for leaving the wet wash in the machine overnight.

Again today I didn't make an appointment with the dentist.

I realized that the show I wanted to see at the Arts Center closed yesterday.

Daydream: Alice and I holding hands, walking down the path behind the barns.

State of mind: Chaos. Unable to decide what to do all morning/afternoon. Gym versus clean apartment versus pumpkin festival versus movie versus beach versus read several articles/long overdue books versus sleep. Tried to sleep after lunch—couldn't relax. After period of "inner debate," forced myself to go to the gym for a couple of hours. (Names I call myself during preceding debate: intelligent, lazy, selfish, selfless, nice, slow, dumb, shy, cute, naïve, jaded, tired.)

Dream: A Nazi general pushes me into a large blue swimming pool. As I swim to the side and attempt to get out, several people at the side of the pool push me back in. The general, wearing his uniform, pulls me into the middle of the water, pushes me under—I escape and the series of actions continues again and again and again. I never escape completely, but I am not drowned either.

Inner debate: Jealousy over one friend's talking to another friend. I feel slighted and wish that I could control my friend's actions—make him react as I want him to. Yet I know that after a while I would grow extremely bored with such a relationship. There would never be any growth.

Dream: Am watching a scene within a scene in which a girl is auditioning for a commercial. It's an ad for perfume, and she attracts both men and women with her sensual smell. Later the girl is at home; she is talking with her mother. She is thrilled that she landed a part in the commercial, yet is worried that the ad is too risqué and will offend friends.

Inner debate: Self-image. Changes from time to time depending on the person or group I happen to be with. At work, quiet, diligent worker; with some, happy, carefree, good ol' boy. With supervisor, hard worker, serious, eager, bust-ass for company. Another role—crazy, unpredictable though congenial young man. At the gym, either loner or joke teller. With my folks, it's still son asking for advice. Concern about appearance. Worry about loss of hair. Have been exercising, jogging, training with weights, watching diet. Seems like slow process. Get down on myself for lack of willpower for eating junk food, empty calories. (Names I call myself: sloppy, weak-willed, lazy, ugly.)

Dream: Am back in my hometown wandering around in the attic and basement of a Methodist church. It's very dark and smells like musty dirt. I see some chairs and funeral wreaths and trunks stored in the cellar and am frightened. In the attic I become lost and cannot find my way out. I wander forever and find myself behind a big pipe organ. I hear the strains of music and can see the congregation before me but they do not see me. I am frightened.

State of mind: Chaos. Running late for date—don't know which shirt to wear—cool enough for jacket?—where are keys?—where is cheapest, closest gas station?—where in hell did I put my wallet?—settle down—you're late—so? You're late. Take it easy.

Inner debate: Office mate at work receives praise for project we both worked on. I sit back, allow her to bask solely in the limelight, while I take a back seat as though I didn't help at all. I even wonder if the supervisor realizes I put in much work on this. I am ashamed of myself for allowing it to continue, yet I don't know how I can tactfully bring it to his attention that I too deserve some credit. Am rather put out with my office mate for not volunteering the fact that I deserve credit also. I feel like a schmuck for not standing up for myself. I realize that I will merely harbor my resentment despite the fact that I realize I should say something. Am down on myself. Am afraid of confrontation. Think maybe it isn't important. Am copping out.

Dream: Am having a fight with a couple of my good friends from my hometown. At first, it is merely verbal—later, the female friend starts to claw at me—I don't want to hit her, but if she doesn't stop, I will have to for my own safety. Next, my male friend is grabbing me, trying to pin me down and hit me. He is stronger than I, and I realize that he will win. I don't want to hit him either, so I continue to struggle with him and attempt to edge away. This seems to go on for hours. I really do want to escape from his grasp and these two people—I feel that my heart will soon break. Finally, I awaken at the alarm.

WHAT'S GOING ON IN THERE?

What is it like to try to capture the Inner Dialogue? Are the voices evasive? Unclear? Did you find time to set aside to listen in? Are you surprised at the number and complexity of voices? At the shouting and contradictions and power plays?

This is the way we humanfolk are—a network, sometimes a tangled one—of voices and opinions. Rather than be put off by the confusing babble, we should feel encouraged at the rich tapestry of our inner lives, at the resources and imagination at our disposal, if we can just get a handle on them. We are not as boring as we feared!

The inner voices can be a positive force: We should encourage them to speak out, learn to revel in their babble and debate, and accept this active dialogue as a way to learn about ourselves, to self-consult, and to solve problems.

8

Who's Talking in There?
Identifying the Inner Voices

WHEN IN PURSUIT of the Inner Enemy, one of the first worthwhile exercises is to monitor the Inner Dialogue to determine exactly who is talking in there and how, to assign each voice a name and enumerate its traits. Naming the voices and learning a bit about their ways is the foundation for more intimate knowledge of the twerp. The ability to isolate each voice is the beginning of a consciousness-raising process that will enable you to fight the Inner Enemy fair and square.

Remember that it is normal to have a number of voices and conflicting opinions, all trying to be heard. Single-mindedness is a myth; we are all of many minds. There isn't one little thing about which we do not have many, many thoughts that overlap and are sometimes downright incompatible. But occasionally the voices are so muddled, so often do they shout each other down, so confused are we by what they are saying, that it feels like one big mess inside.

Everyone has a different number of voices that show up at different times and speak in different ways and have varying amounts of power. To learn to cope with the Inner Enemy, we must try to identify each voice that pipes in on our Inner Dialogues, and see what it says and when. Only then can we learn to call on each voice as needed, only then can we talk back. Only then can we try to reorganize that inner power structure.

Some of the voices will turn up almost as soon as you start the search. They are the familiar ones that always have something to say—about your looks, your eating habits, your sex life. Others pop up rarely, only in the most specialized situations—in a crisis, at Christmas or other holidays, on the rare day you spend away from the kids.

Be prepared to accumulate evidence slowly and to keep records or notes of twerp visits and conversations. At this stage little analysis is necessary. The task is only to listen in, to observe and accumulate data. Later come interpretation, analysis, and twerp-control learning.

Following are descriptions of a number of voices; each represents a different aspect of one's inner life. Each has a different level of power and influences.

It is clear from these descriptions that there is a common thread that unites all the enemy voices: They want you to stay put, to maintain the status quo. They are interested in security and safety. And the common denominator of the ally voices? Action, growth, support, change. Enemy voices seek failure; allies, success. Enemy voices say, "Stop"; ally voices say, "Go."

You may or may not recognize each voice as a member of your Inner Parliament. But the descriptions will help you identify some of your own voices or trigger your memory of others not described here. The voices described herein have corny names and quite rigid descriptions to make them easy to recognize. Your own may be variations or combinations of these characters, and the names may not fit. But use these capsule dossiers as a takeoff point to pick out and itemize

your voices; add to the list any additional ones that are peculiar to you. Be sure and give them names—the more vivid the
better—since this makes it easier to point them out and talk
back to them.

ENEMY VOICES

The Spoiler: This voice is the wet blanket of the group. It can
be counted on to show up when you're having a good time—
too good a time, it thinks. This voice is a pleasure stealer.
When you're on vacation, finally, and are winding down from
the pace of your hectic life, it reminds you of things you forgot to do, or itemizes the work waiting for you at home, or it
worries that the house will burn down. As you shed your
cares at a party with friends, you are suddenly overcome by a
feeling of dread, a premonition of some unnameable disaster.
When you receive a promotion, the Spoiler pipes up with all
sorts of reasons why you don't deserve it. When you win a
race, complete a difficult task, enjoy a new friend's company,
when things are going just too well, the Spoiler will come
along to take the fun out of it.

The Goof-off: The Goof-off always has persuasive arguments
for neglecting your obligations. "C'mon," it says, "you're entitled to a good time." So you put off the work you have to
do; or you don't get around to writing the article you'd promised, or making the phone calls, or doing the planting or
cleaning—all with the encouragement of the Goof-off. This
voice convinces you that you're so smart you can get the
work done in no time, or so beloved no one will mind if you
shirk your responsibilities. It all seems like great fun. You go
shopping, or play golf, or read magazines—until the deadline
comes around, or until you realize you have sabotaged your

chances for a promotion or alienated your family and friends because you didn't pitch in. The sweet-talking Goof-off loves to engineer things cleverly so that you don't accomplish what you could.

The Doubter: "You'll never be able to do that." "You're getting in over your head." "That's just too difficult." The Doubter has a very low opinion of your abilities. It's a wonder you can get through the day without making a terrible blunder. It's a wonder you have any friends, that you can keep your job. In the names of caution and reason, this voice will keep you from attempting anything new on the grounds that you just aren't up to it, or that it doesn't want to see you hurt. Listen to this voice enough and you'll stay stuck right where you are, until you're afraid to try anything new—even something exotic on a restaurant menu.

The Pessimist: This is the voice of doom and gloom, a bottomless well of frightening predictions and bad news. It never expects anything good to come of anything or anyone. You will never get out of debt. Your son will probably flunk out of school and end up a bum. There will be no snow when you go skiing next weekend. The bus will be late. The new neighbors will turn out to be bores. You won't enjoy the movie. Aside from stealing your rightful pleasures in life, the pessimist serves the function of giving you an excuse *not* to do, *not* to try, *not* to care, *not* to count on, *not* to want things.

The Overindulger: At first, this voice seems like a good buddy. It always wants more for you—more good food, more to drink, another party, some recreational drugs, more clothes, more fun. The Overindulger is not about to restrain you from going off your diet—devil-may-care, it urges you to enjoy yourself; besides, you can make up for it tomorrow. And what's wrong with a few extra drinks at a party? It's the weekend and you've worked hard. If your friends don't like it

... well, they're such stiffs, they don't know how to have a good time. Smoking—it relaxes you, it's a habit, you shouldn't be intimidated by a lot of bleeding-heart propaganda. The Overindulger walks along with its arm around your shoulder, telling you what a terrific fellow you are. It is an insidious voice, hard to spot and hard to say no to.

The Bumbler: This one can never do anything right. Every day you get up and dress and go to work like a grown-up. But suddenly today the Bumbler turns up. You oversleep. Drop the toothpaste cap. Scald yourself in the shower. Spill coffee. Don't have change for the bus. Knock the telephone off your desk. What's the matter—a big lunch date? Was today the day you were going to ask for a raise? Is there a deadline? The Bumbler will make you feel clumsy and incompetent, just when you thought you were doing pretty well, just when you need to be at the top of your form.

The Knife-Twister: Here is a real creep. As if you don't have enough problems, or do enough things to get in your own way, or feel bad enough when something goes wrong, you have the Knife-Twister to add to your woes. This is the voice that won't let you off the hook if you do something wrong, no matter how small or innocent the offense. It can be something as simple as forgetting to turn the lights off when you leave the house: "How could you do that? Don't you ever think before you act? Do you think electricity's free? Isn't there an energy crisis? How selfish." Heaven forbid you should do something more serious. The Knife-Twister will spend years browbeating you about it, rubbing salt in your wounds. It's a very effective tactic, great for lowering self-esteem and creating anxiety over insoluble, long-past situations, when you could be doing something constructive.

The Nurse: This is another voice that seems to be a friend. The nurse is always fussing over you, telling you to take it easy, not to work too hard, not to think about things that confuse or upset you. The nurse will pamper you, encourage you to stay home when you have a little headache, make excuses for your behavior. Unfortunately, the nurse only wants you to be weak and dependent, and persuades you to avoid responsibilities and challenges that you would be better off facing.

The Belittler: This is the voice that turns your dreams and accomplishments to ashes. "So you finally got up the nerve to tell Allan that he should share the housework. Big deal. You should have done it a long time ago." "What in the world do you want to study acting for? You'll starve. It'll take years before you get any parts. You're not exactly a natural." "At your age you should be making more money." "Nancy's going to think you're weird if you wear that shirt." "You call that a soufflé?" "Why do you waste your time with such a useless hobby?" The Belittler makes it hard to take pride in your abilities and discourages your interest in trying new things.

The Scaredy-cat: This character is afraid of everything. Afraid you'll get sick. Afraid you'll fall down. Doesn't want you to take that long drive. Afraid it'll rain. Afraid to buy a house if there's a chance that real-estate values will fall. Afraid to call a new friend to make a date. Afraid there's going to be war. It's a sure thing that listening to this voice will raise your anxiety level and keep you sticking close to home.

The Love-Crusher: This one is a big troublemaker. It not only brings out all your fears about other people's love and the possibility of rejection, but it helps those fears come true. This voice is always questioning whether your friends *really* care for you, always finding evidence that your spouse doesn't love you so much anymore, that your children are indifferent, that the world is a hostile place, that your coworker is out to get you. This voice is so convincing that soon you'll be acting as though it knew the real truth. Perhaps then you'll retreat from your mate, or act hurt and put upon in front of the kids, or act less friendly to your coworker, or badger your friends for proof of their devotion, testing their love, expecting the unreasonable. And then perhaps you'll get your wish and they *won't* care so much anymore.

The Procrastinator: This voice is a classic character in the Inner Enemy repertoire. What better, more effective way to stagnate, to be unable to grow and move on than simply not to do what you are supposed to do? Artist's block and writer's block are classic examples—and illustrative of a typical human paradox. Who works more intensely to create—to forge something new—than the artist? And who therefore is most beset by the Inner Enemy, furious and frightened at such attempts to grow beyond the limitations it tries to impose? The Procrastinator employs all kinds of insidious tactics, from sidetracking you with unimportant concerns and tasks, to putting you through the agony of sitting and staring at your work for hours or days on end—tense, anxious, practically paralyzed, unable to do a thing.

ALLY VOICES

The Adventurer: When you want to try something new, to make a change, to explore, the Adventurer is right with you. It helps you not get bogged down in unproductive doubts, groundless fears, endless questioning. The Adventurer enjoys trying new food, meeting new people, learning new things. It reassures you of the benefits and rewards of success and the pleasures of trying. It encourages you to go out on a limb, to take the risks—however grand or humble—that will help you get where you want to go.

The Comforter: When you are having a hard time, when you have made a mistake or failed at something, the Comforter will soothe your frazzled nerves and reassure you that you're all right. The Comforter rescues you from self-recrimination. The Comforter licks your wounds when you've been hurt. It helps you take care of yourself, go easy on yourself, get over what's troubling you and move on.

The Voice of Reason: It is all too easy to get carried away with foolish plans, say something hurtful, drink too much, drive dangerously, dwell on unproductive thoughts. This level-headed voice keeps you from going to extremes in your behavior, feelings, and action, keeps you from pushing to unreasonable conclusions, dangerous limits. It is your safety net when you're tempted to go too far, your rescuer from the taunts and goading of the Inner Enemy. The Voice of Reason monitors what you do to see that you make healthy choices and tries, with common sense, to offset those voices that would drive you to do things that might harm you or set up overblown expectations of your abilities or strengths.

The Good Buddy: This voice is the companion and confidant of your inner life. It understands you and wants the best for you, is sympathetic to your dreams, your feelings, your concerns. It is this voice to whom you confide day-to-day issues and major undertakings; it is your companion when you mull over a problem, try to reach a decision. The Good Buddy will talk back to enemies and critics.

The Optimist: To the Optimist the world is an OK place, life is good, and everything is going to work out all right. The

Optimist won't let you get bogged down in gloomy predictions, negative scenarios; it won't let you give up. This voice keeps you thinking positively about your work, your friends and family, and especially yourself. During difficult times the Optimist convinces you that you will prevail and that a good solution will be found. It doesn't let you back down in anticipation of a bad outcome, and it overrides doubts, bad news, dire predictions.

The Fan: In the eyes of the Fan, you are something special. The Fan is a loyal supporter who sees all the good, strong, positive traits in you and points them out at every opportunity. "You remember so much of what you read." "What a healthy appetite." "Your new girlfriend is going to love it when you play the piano for her." "Your willpower on this diet is impressive." "You're hot stuff!" "It's great that you painted the kitchen." The Fan believes in you and what you can do, and its cheers and compliments can overcome the doubts and criticism of powerful enemies.

The Go-getter: The Go-getter gets things done—no procrastination, no doubts, no second-guessing, no putting off till tomorrow. Whether getting your laundry done, painting a picture, studying for exams, washing the dishes, or launching a new career as a rock star, the Go-getter sees that you accomplish what you set out to do. This voice supports your ambitions and helps you to realize them.

The Dreamer: This is the creative one, full of ideas, new approaches, innovative techniques, wild fantasies, blissful daydreams. The Dreamer helps you to look at things in new ways, lets you dare aspire to high and difficult goals. It keeps you from getting bogged down in unimportant trivia, from being stymied by overpracticality. It seeks new, different, personal solutions to problems, whether it is a new way to serve hamburgers, to be able to work a four-day week, to write a symphony, or to keep your kids from drinking.

Using this list as an example, make your own cast of inner characters. Give them names and write down whatever you know about them. For example:

"Whenever I call home, the Love-Crusher is sure to turn up and say, 'But why call? It doesn't matter to them if they hear from you.'"

"The Oaf's tactic is to have me go to work with two different-colored socks on."

"My Procrastinator's tactic is to convince me that I have plenty of time to get my work done, so there's no rush."

On this first go-around you may not be able to identify many voices, and you may not be able to pin down much hard information about them. Time, and new tactics for getting at the twerp, will give you more culprits and more information. For the time being, this list is the basis for helping you confront the Inner Enemy.

ANALYZING THE VOICES

WHO WAS THAT MASKED STRANGER?

Did you recognize the voices that turned up? Do any of the voices in your Inner Dialogue match the descriptions given? Were there new faces—previously unrecognized commentators hiding in there till you drove them from their lair? As times goes by, have you become better able to distinguish one from the other?

Did you recognize any ex-selves: the kid who used to be a bully? Who blushed when called on in class? Who hated to have to be chosen for teams? Who worried that his parents wouldn't come home from their vacation? Who was afraid to admit he liked to play with the girls? Who never had his homework ready? Who liked to read alone in his room?

What about people in your past? Did any of the voices sound uncannily like one of your parents? Or a teacher, neighbor, or clergyman?

WHAT DO THEY HAVE TO SAY FOR THEMSELVES?

How do the voices talk? Are some calm and rational, full of glib, logical arguments about what an asshole you are, about how risky (or foolish or useless) your behavior is? Do some voices shout and act irrationally just to get attention? Is there a double-talker, first saying one thing and then another in the hope of confusing or deceiving you? Do some voices whisper so you can't quite pick out what they're saying? Perhaps their tactics vary—from cunning to bluntness, from brute strength to reason.

Are there prominent, repeated voices? Familiar refrains that echo over and over again a litany that never varies? What about round robins—the same old argument between the same old parties over and over, months, years on end?

And what about friendly voices? Does anyone have good things to say?

FRIEND OR FOE?

A useful exercise is to go back over your list of voices and determine which of them belong in your ally camp and which are on the twerp's side. Is each voice for you or against you? In favor of moving ahead or hanging back?

Make a two-column list with allies on one side and enemies on the other.

Allies	Enemies

How does the list shape up? Are there more voices on one side than on the other? Which are the most powerful voices? The weakest? Is there a balance?

Go over the list to see what kinds of enemies you *don't* have; this will help you to identify healthy, relatively twerp-free areas. The same with allies: What kinds of friends are missing?

WHO'S IN CHARGE HERE?

It is helpful to determine what form of government is operating. When you're thinking something over, or when your mind is wandering, is there an orderly presentation of thoughts? Do the voices seem to speak in turn, or is there chaos? Is there a balance of positive and negative opinions? Sad and happy thoughts? Fearful and brave ones? Does it seem to be a democratic process, or is there a little dictator who shouts everyone down? Does there seem to be open discussion and fair debate? Do filibusters get going that no one seems able to stop? Are there pairs of voices or coalitions that apparently always oppose each other? Who wins? Is someone in charge: Do you have the ability—at some times or all the time—to tune in to whichever inner consultants are most useful at the moment, or do the voices control you? Is there a monitor who is fair about giving everyone a chance to speak, or do some voices get shoved aside? In a debate can you tell which voices are against you and which are allied with your best interests?

9

Twerp Alert: Identifying Where, When, and How the Inner Enemy Operates

NOW THAT YOU KNOW who the players are, you need to know when and where they are on stage and how they act. Once you know when the Inner Enemy shows up and under what conditions, you can be prepared for its entrance and it will have less impact. When you are familiar with its arenas of operation, you can dilute the Inner Enemy's monopoly in these areas of your life. With skills to help you fight fair with yourself, you can learn to delay the Inner Enemy, talk back to it, overrule it, make fun of it, placate it, muster your allies against it. This can be compared to a search-and-destroy operation. In ferreting out its pockets of influence, you beard the enemy in its lair. You de-claw it, demystify it, detoxify it. You neutralize its acid effect. The power of twerp and ally equalizes.

RECOGNIZING THE TWERP'S TERRITORIES

Most people have areas in their lives in which they are confident and productive. When functioning in these areas, they operate efficiently, things get accomplished. They have ideas, problems get solved. They enjoy themselves. Untroubled by tension and doubts, they are productive. One woman's strength is her home life. She feels good running the house, taking care of the children. She gets things done and doesn't worry unduly about the kids or second-guess how to handle the day-to-day crises and logistics.

Another woman is supersuccessful at her job. She is confident of her abilities, she works well with her coworkers, she doesn't feel threatened by the competition for promotions, and she has her own plans for moving up in the company. She loves the challenge of new projects.

But if people have areas of confidence in which they take pride and pleasure, they have others in which they feel unsure and afraid. The woman who is a confident homemaker and mother is terrified of cocktail parties and community activities, of meeting her husband's clients or her kids' teachers. She worries that she will have nothing to say. She has convinced herself that she is dowdy and unfashionable, that everyone else is much more sophisticated than she. She envisions going to parties and standing alone, unable to start a conversation, or she tries to talk to someone and stammers, or that person becomes so bored he or she can't wait to get away.

The woman who is so confident in her work has a disastrous love life. Poised and articulate on the job, she has no confidence in her attractiveness and is riddled with doubts about her femininity. A single woman living in a large city, she is afraid and unwilling to "compete" for dates. Normally self-possessed, she is a wallflower at the occasional cocktail party she forces herself to attend. She persuades herself that she would rather spend a quiet evening at home than be out someplace with people she neither knows nor cares for. Her occasional dates are often so uncomfortable that neither party wants a repeat. In some part of her Inner Dialogue, a voice tells her not to worry, not to rush, the right man will come along and "discover" her.

Another reason for knowing the twerp's ways is that the accumulated evidence will enable you to separate fact from fiction. This is a vital consideration in dealing with the twerp, for it is a master of self-crazymaking techniques. It will deny your experience, contradict your memories: "No, that's not how it happened." It will rewrite history, alter facts unmercifully. When the twerp denies your perceptions, you have nowhere to turn for confirmation. When the twerp insists over and over that it is right, we eventually defer to its opinions. We come to believe that we *do* have the ugliest nose in the world. We believe that the fact that we have "too much" pubic hair makes us unfit for sexual pleasure. We agree with the twerp that we don't deserve the promotion, or that we should stay with an unloving spouse, or that it's all right to be a little late, or that our children don't care about us, or that we're too weird to be lovable.

The women cited above came to believe in the twerp's perceptions. The first woman *lived her life* under the impression that she was dowdy and uninteresting and should stay in the kitchen. The other woman *lived her life* as though she were unattractive, unfeminine, not up to snuff at the dating game.

You too probably have your comfortable and uncomfortable areas. You have probably noticed that there are times when the twerp is quiet and hasn't much to say, other times when it is raucous and obnoxious and impossible to shut up. Sometimes it's quiet because you have enough real worries of your own and don't need its added bedevilment to keep you sufficiently miserable. Other times the twerp is quiet because whatever you are involved in isn't one of its pet concerns— you are functioning in an area that is healthier and relatively twerp-free. But there are other areas where it will pipe up every time.

Also, be aware that the twerp will move around. When formerly fertile ground dries up and it cannot convince you of its viewpoint anymore, it will find another arena in which you are vulnerable. Andy's story:

"When I was a young man, my Inner Enemy picked on me constantly about my height. 'You're short,' 'You have to be better than the next guy,' 'No woman likes a little pipsqueak.' I spent endless energy proving to people that my height didn't make any difference. I always had to be the first, the best, the wittiest. I had to try and sleep with every woman who crossed my path, and brag to my men friends about it. I wore elevator shoes. Everything. As I grew older, after years and years of this behavior, my Inner Enemy must have felt it couldn't get another rise out of me on this one— there was just no evidence to support the contention that my height made a difference. Even *I* had to admit that my height wasn't affecting my life one way or another, except as I chose to find it important. So now that I'm successful, established, retired—not a pipsqueak loser—my Inner Enemy has shifted to fresh territory: 'You're not really a success,' 'You're not really important,' 'No one will remember your contribution twenty years from now.' I get invited to lecture and give workshops at prestigious universities, I'm quoted regularly in my profession, my books are best-sellers, and the little voice keeps saying, 'But you'll be found out. Your reputation won't last.' Again in total contradiction to the facts of my life."

Eventually the realities of our lives, our repeated successes and accomplishments, and the outward verification of them, have their impact on us and force us to reconsider the harsh and heavy-handed opinion of the twerp. Slowly we start believing in the view of ourselves for which we actually have evidence, and we overrule the opinion of the Inner Enemy. But it is just at this time—when we are successful and satisfied with ourselves—that we must watch out, for the twerp will certainly find a new area to infect, often an unexpected one, unpredictable and without precedent. In Andy's case, there was "historical" reason for the twerp picking on Andy's height: He had been teased about it—and his parents had worried about it out loud—when he was a child. When the twerp shifted to the arena of Andy's reputation in his field, there was no historical reason—he had always been appreciated and acclaimed in his work. But perhaps because he was retired and his work was behind him and there was little he could do to add to it or to change it at that point, the twerp felt it would have Andy in a situation where he truly felt powerless to fight back.

TWERP ARENAS

The major arenas of twerp activity are discussed below. It would be impossible to enumerate the quirks and idiosyncrasies of the twerp, for each person's Inner Enemy is custom-tailored; no two are exactly alike. Probably no two are remotely alike. But under each category are several examples and anecdotes about the way in which the twerp might exert its influence. Also in each section are questions to help you identify where the Inner Enemy wields power in your life— and when and how. This and the information gathered in Chapters 7 and 8 are the basis for filling out the Twerp Alert Report at the end of this chapter.

BODY IMAGE

This is one of the twerp's favorite arenas. It can really get its hooks in because it has proof: Just look in the mirror! That's some ugly nose! A disgusting pimple! The fattest thighs this side of the Mississippi! Year after year, that same ugly nose, those same repulsive thighs!

Picking on how we look seems to be a universal twerp activity. It loves to latch on to one flaw or to a few very specific ones—and magnify them and harp on them and bring them repeatedly to our attention. This practice is not limited to the plain or average-looking person. Dr. Bach's many years of experience with Hollywood actors and actresses showed him that beautiful people are by no means exempt: All of them without exception found fault with, and were plagued by, flaws that seemed insignificant, even invisible.

Lewis Jablonsky, a pioneer and longtime practitioner in the field of psychotherapy, reports that thousands of people in his workshops have done his body-image exercise—the purpose of which is to make people more comfortable with their bodies—and not one has failed to find faults. Very few people felt lucky or grateful or superior about their looks. They saw only the warts.

The twerp makes it hard to keep a clear perspective on your looks because it doesn't see the whole picture. It not only focuses on physical attributes while ignoring other things, it has a habit of picking out one or two flaws and blowing them up to gargantuan proportions, continually calling your attention to body "downers," those flaws that eventually overshadow all the positive aspects of your looks. You dwell morbidly on these twerp-induced hooks until they influence your behavior. A man develops the habit of self-consciously turning his head a certain way to hide a blemish he feels is ugly. A woman is so traumatized by the fact that her figure doesn't match fashion ideals that she avoids situations in which she has to wear a bathing suit. A man's intense discomfort over his "small" penis or "too much" body hair keeps him from having sex and eventually even from dating. And none of these fears is rooted in a realistic evaluation of physical flaws. An inordinate amount of worry and thought is spent dwelling on them; an inordinate amount of behavior is influenced by them.

"Sometimes I go shopping for clothes and if I'm not feeling good about myself that day, nothing will look good on me. I'll try on dozens of things, and each one will look worse than the one before. By the end of the shopping trip, I'll be almost in tears over how terrible I look. The same thing happens often when I have someplace special to go—a party, a date. I'll try on everything I own, yet nothing will look right—even things which I've felt fine in before. In desperation, I'll settle for something very plain or shapeless and feel unattractive all evening."

"I've become obsessed by the fact that I have too much body hair. As a teenager my buddies used to tease me about it—they'd call me "He-man" or "Ape-man," but it never seemed to bother me. Then in the past few years I find myself looking around at all the guys on the beach, envying the ones with sleek bodies and light hair. I find the hairy men repugnant and continually compare them to myself. I find myself staring at my body, hating that I have hair on my back, or too much hair on my chest and the back of my hands. I've even toyed with having some of it removed, but that seems wrong, too. Sometimes I'll leave my shirt on so as not to display my hair. And I'm very sensitive about the subject with women. If I start to date someone new, I'll very surreptitiously try to check out her 'preference'—though to be truthful, as far as I know, no woman I've ever been with seems to feel that it matters."

A person's entire life—every social encounter, every decision, every opinion—can be colored or diminished by his twerp's exaggerated perception of a flaw that few people even notice.

Where does your twerp attack your body? What does it have to say about how you look? Look at yourself in a full-length mirror and see what the twerp has to say. Make a list of every complaint you hear. Are they familiar refrains? What doesn't the twerp like? Have there been any changes—has it given up chiding you about being overweight and now picks on your scrawny muscles or your dry skin? Do you think it's fair-minded criticism? Is its opinion level-headed? Is it pretty much in keeping with what others think?

When does it do this? When you look in the mirror in the morning? When you're getting ready for a date? When you're sitting across from your date? When you're in bed with your spouse or lover? While looking at fashion magazines? When you're trying on clothes?

Perhaps the twerp is very indirect—it has you wear baggy clothes so no one notices you. Or if someone compliments you on how you look, you think he is lying. Or the twerp has convinced you that looks count for everything.

And what kind of comment does it make? Direct insults—"You look so fat in those pants!"; "Your eyes are too close together." Or innuendos—"Your friend Pat is sure a doll." Or "Why do you read those fashion magazines?" (when you don't even look remotely like those models).

What about allies? Does your body have friends and supporters? Who speaks up and says, "You look gorgeous," or "That exercise class is paying off," or "What a great dress this is on you," or "Your hair looks great in curls." Do these friends ever challenge the twerp? Ever overpower it?

Are there situations in which you usually feel confident about your looks? Does this confidence have to do with the presence of certain people, with the kind of clothes you're wearing? Do you feel good out on a date with one person but unattractive in comparison with a group of your peers? What physical attributes do you feel best about?

Self-care

Here's an area in which the twerp's behavior can be very deceptive, for we look at many of our actions as self-indulgent and self-centered when in fact they're not very good for us at all. After all, the twerp doesn't want us to take good care of ourselves. It would just like us to think we do. And if we feel at all guilty about it, so much the better.

Some people find it extremely uncomfortable to be alone. They lack resources and the sense of self-worth to keep themselves company, and the empty time alone favors twerp takeover. Such people feel that somehow their loneliness is not a result of circumstances, it's their fault. If they were more likable, they think, they wouldn't be alone. They can't find anything to do on their own. Time passes slowly; they stew over their plight. Some, to avoid facing their inner demons and their emptiness, will go to any lengths not to be alone. These people develop bad autohedonic habits. They go out every night, often with people they don't care about, often drinking or taking drugs, to places that are equally meaningless. They join clubs and committees, filling up the time so they can just go home and go to bed and, with luck, to sleep.

Painful loneliness is the twerp's work. People who cannot be with themselves often seek therapy. But this is a somewhat paradoxical place to learn how to be alone, since the very nature of therapy is being with an understanding and comforting other. Patients unconsciously are buying regularly scheduled contact time with an intelligent, sympathetic listener and conversationalist. In this situation the therapist must not allow the patient to become dependent on their time together and must address directly the problem of his inability to be alone.

People who care for themselves respect and have a good opinion of themselves. People lacking in self-care find fault everywhere. They judge every move, every word. They make generalizations about their behavior. If they forget something once, they label *themselves,* not their behavior, forgetful. If they do something thoughtless once, they label *themselves,* not their behavior, unkind or selfish. And the labels have their effect: "I am mean," "I am stupid," "I am ugly": Who wants to hang around with such a person?

There are people who don't feel they are witty or attractive. They are neglectful of themselves—of their health, their sleep, their need for friends or for pleasant surroundings. They don't want to pamper themselves if they feel sick. If they are alone, they don't take the trouble to cook a nice meal for themselves or go out to a restaurant. They feel guilty if they buy new clothes or spend money on themselves. "I should save this for the children's school clothes." "Hiring a babysitter is a terrible extravagance."

For others, lack of self-care shows up as overindulgence. What could be more destructive than drinking too much, staying up all night partying and taking drugs, sleeping with a different person five times a week, spending more money than one earns, eating rich food—or junk food—every night of the week?

"I lead a very busy life. I work hard, belong to several active organizations, have a big circle of friends to keep up with. Lately I've become aware of how stressed I feel and how it's taking its toll on me. Several times in the last year I've tried to learn relaxation techniques of various kinds. None of them works for me. I just can't seem to let go, to shut down the inner babble, to turn my attention away from the thoughts that crowd into my head. Usually I'm very good at learning new things, but when I try this I can feel the battle going on in my head. It's as if the Inner Enemy doesn't want me to escape from these troubling feelings."

"It is so hard for me to spend an evening alone. It always seems that I have so much to do—phone calls to make, correspondence to catch up on, little projects around the house, my needlework. Yet when I do stay home, I feel nervous. I'll keep raiding the refrigerator. I'll read a magazine that normally wouldn't hold my attention for more than ten minutes. I'll pace around the house, straightening things here and there. Then I'll worry about why I feel so out of sorts. And then, I'll feel very tired—very early—and go to bed without having accomplished anything, without having enjoyed the hours to myself."

First of all, what do you think of yourself? Are you an OK person? Or are you mean or boring or weak? Who says so— your friends? Lovers? Family? Coworkers? Or is this the twerp's humble opinion?

Do you spend a good deal of time thinking about yourself and your life? How? Do you make positive, constructive plans for the future? Do you rehash fond memories or past accomplishments? Or is that time spent brooding, wondering what's wrong with you, feeling tense and anxious about your plans, playing over and over again the mental tape of past failures or shortcomings? How are you sleeping? Do you have sweet dreams? Or nightmares?

Are you treating yourself well? Eating properly? Getting enough sleep? Spending some time at leisure, doing things you want to do? Do you enjoy yourself when you're alone? Or are you lonely unless there are others around?

Do you have any habits that seem to bug you? Smoking too much? Or drinking? Or using drugs? Or spending too much money?

WORK AND PLAY

This is a most interesting area for twerp scouting, because it involves our unique skills and talents, goals and pleasures. In work and at play, we have the opportunity to speak up for our dreams, our individuality and independence. And it is in sidetracking or sabotaging these goals that we often turn up the twerp.

There are all kinds of tactics it can use to keep you from growing in your work, from enjoying your leisure.

It can make you fearful of failing at your work; it can

cause you to hang back, to play safe, perhaps even to spend your time at a job that is safe but which doesn't use your talents. The twerp may keep you in a job out of fear. Or it may let you waste your time in a field that is really not what you like or are best at. Worse yet, it may let you be successful at this sham career.

When you do make progress, the Inner Enemy may cause you to sabotage that success indirectly, as Ellen's story illustrates:

"I can't believe it but I finally have a job I like. Keeping regular hours has never been my thing, but I managed to get in more or less at nine. Then a couple of weeks ago a co-worker told me our boss was really a stickler for punctuality. So I said to myself, 'Well, I'd better make a point of getting in on time.' However, the results have been exactly the opposite. Somehow I'm never on time anymore. I set the alarm, then fall back to sleep, or rationalize why it's OK to sleep a few minutes longer. Or I suddenly need to fix an elaborate breakfast. Or there's a long story in the paper I must read. Then I go to work in sheer terror of being late again, sure I'm going to be fired. And I really want this job."

Lack of confidence in your work or play can undermine your pleasure, can make you want to avoid competition. For some it's a barrier that must be overcome day after day.

"The way I play competitive games tells me a good deal about my lack of self-esteem. If I'm behind I'll battle like hell to catch up. But if I manage to get ahead, I'll lose my concentration and let up on my efforts—almost imperceptibly—until the match gets close again. Then if it really gets down to the wire—the last game, the last few points—where it looks like I might actually win—then I really go to pieces. Suddenly my serve will completely desert me. My whole body tightens and I'll make outrageous mistakes. Then I'll win back the points and keep the match alive. I'm so aware of what's going on—it's like a demon inside me—and sometimes I can fight back. Other times it's too much for me. The demon wins and I blow another tennis game that I should have won. And *then*, I'm down on myself for losing."

For some people the very act of having fun can be stressful. They have learned that if things are going well, if they are too successful or having too good a time, they will bring something on themselves to turn it to ashes. They may get a feeling of dread, of free-floating anxiety. They may have sudden feelings of guilt or reminders of all the things they haven't done or of past "sins." Perhaps they get sick, or have an accident. Whatever it is, so frightening are the consequences of success or fun that people hold themselves in check: They're afraid to laugh too loudly, to revel in their success, to feel too much pleasure. They're always looking over their shoulder, always waiting for the ax to fall. "It can't last," they say.

The pressure to be acceptable to others, to be successful at and enjoy the things our families and communities uphold, can be devastating. Many people are so heavily indoctrinated by their environment to pursue a particular way of life that they aren't even aware of having made any choices, or of perhaps having given up something important in the dim past. Some who may have fought for their own ideas and interests and pleasures often felt so unacceptable, so ostracized for their deviation, that they finally succumbed. Perhaps they gave in, in weary defeat. Perhaps they came to doubt their inner voices and to believe in the course prescribed for them. Perhaps they weighed the price to be paid for their individuality and made a conscious choice for the love and acceptance of others.

* * *

"It's always been a battle for me to do what's important to me. I grew up in a home where there were no books or music, where art and culture were considered effete and phony. Though my interest in art was encouraged by a family friend and by teachers, I was made to feel weird and different. It was hinted that I wouldn't have friends, wouldn't be popular, wouldn't find a husband—all the things that were important. I was told I wouldn't be happy. I must have believed it, because I put a lot of energy into trying to be attractive and likable, helpful and popular. Yet there was always a voice inside me saying, 'There's nothing wrong with the way you are,' 'You're a good artist,' 'It's not the most important thing in the world to be pretty,' 'You can get a job, have a career as an artist.' This inner dialogue went on constantly; these two choices were always being presented. Even now, almost twenty years out of school, I still feel a prisoner of this conflict, I am still constantly fighting with myself to do one thing or the other. I've had quite a successful career—as a graphic designer, as a designer of craft work, as a writer and a packager of craft books, lately as a writer of books on many subjects. Yet what I've always wanted to do is be a 'real' artist—to paint and draw and make prints. I let everything get in the way so I don't do this. I rationalize that what I do is fine, that I enjoy the success and the money I get in my present career, that I can't give up the money for the risk of painting, that I might fail—i.e., maybe I'm not any good. I know this isn't true, but I've avoided making this important change for years. Somehow I must still believe that if I do what I really want, it will be unacceptable. I won't be happy and will lose the love of those I care about."

Perfectionism can be another form of procrastination: Often it arises out of fear of failure. What if the writing, the painting, the report turn out to be no good? People become so afraid of risking failure, of chancing another blow to their self-esteem, that they avoid the risk by *not doing the work*. They become perpetual students, needing one more course, one more degree. Or the barrier to overcome may be fear of success. If they accomplish what they set out to do, will they lose the love of those who tried to dissuade them? Will they bring disaster down on their heads?

"I sometimes spend days without putting a word on paper. I'll sit at my desk, staring at the blank page, but unable to write. Before I sit down, I'll give myself a pep talk, try and convince myself to write just anything, it doesn't have to be great, just a rough draft that I can work from. But I can't seem to get started. I need a perfect first sentence. I need to have the whole idea, or chapter, clear in my head, have to be sure of all the points I want to touch on. I'll keep turning to things I should read to help me write, or to confirm an opinion. Soon the whole day will be gone. I'm a nervous wreck, my stomach is in knots. I feel terrible about myself and start lecturing myself about how I'm going to work the *next* day. Meanwhile, I've set such impossible standards for myself that I can't get anything done. I can't bear to write a mediocre draft, to compose less-than-beautiful sentences, as though they reflect on me, confirm some negative opinion of myself."

First of all, is life interesting for you? Do you have things you like to do? Places to go? Enough money? Books to read? Things to learn? Or are you often bored? Does life seem dull? Not much to do? Everything's a drag? No challenges? Too many challenges?

Do you have work that you enjoy, that is challenging and uses your talents and abilities? Or is your work boring? Or beneath your talents, perhaps not even in a field in which you are particularly interested or excel? What would you really like to be doing? What's stopping you? (Be specific.)

How do you handle competition? Do you worry about

promotions, about getting ahead? Do you enjoy the struggle or avoid it? Does your twerp act up when you try and win? Is it more quiet, more comfortable when you lose? Or does a different but equally scathing voice show up then?

FRIENDS AND FAMILY

The twerp is not crazy about our having loving friends and family, a network of supporting, validating others. After all, we hardly deserve them, we're so unattractive and schlumpy and unlovable. Besides, supportive friends and family contradict the opinion of ourselves the twerp's been at such pains to have us believe.

As long as the Inner Enemy has us hanging on to our low self-esteem and poor self-image, we'll never give true credit to our friends' or family's feelings about us, never be fully and trustingly able to give to them. As long as we live on past ideas of our worth, we won't trust present estimates.

The twerp may encourage us to have friends who are not good for our self-esteem, who are critical, who trivialize our interests and aspirations, who undercut our accomplishments—who, in short, echo the voice of the Inner Enemy.

When we have supportive friends and family, the twerp may hint that they're imposters—if they really knew us, they wouldn't love us. Or it may keep us distant from loving friends and family, fearful of intimacy and dependence.

The old-fashioned, conformist Inner Enemy may encourage us to have expectations for our children which override their true natures and desires, and the twerp will make us angry at these unmet expectations and guilty about our feelings.

"My husband and I are very upset that our daughter is such a tomboy. She spends all her time out in the yard, up and down the street, playing baseball, riding bikes, roller-skating, climbing the hill, exploring the new house under construction. She's the only girl. She has girlfriends, but she's never interested in their games for very long. Jim finds it very upsetting and thinks it unattractive in a girl. He likes to see her wear a dress once in a while. We just want to see her happy, and it's going to be very hard for her to have friends as she grows up."

"Ever since my marriage broke up five years ago, I have a terrible fear of losing my children—of their lives being out of my control, of my ex-wife telling them stories about me, of them preferring their more comfortable life with her. In my sane moments, I know that I've always been an attentive father and that the kids love me very much. But sometimes I'll think one of my daughters looks unhappy or withdrawn, or is saying something I take to mean she doesn't care for me. And then everything she does seems to confirm this impression. I'm sure she doesn't love me, sure my ex-wife has pulled some trick, sure I've done something wrong. I'll dwell all day, all weekend, on the situation, pulling back and being withdrawn myself, hurt and angry, spoiling our time together. And once it starts, once I find that first telltale sign that I'm not loved, I don't seem to be able to stop myself from blowing it up into a major disaster. Even as I scold myself and tell myself to behave like an adult, I keep digging in deeper and deeper—as though I don't want to believe in their love, don't feel I deserve it. I engineer my own rejections."

"My husband pointed out to me the other day that every time he comes up and puts his arm around me or stops to spend a couple of quiet minutes with me, I suddenly remember something I *must* do: put the roast in the oven, walk the dog, write down our son's dentist appointment. It's a way of showing him how busy and responsible I am and how much I do for him while undercutting his attempts to be close to me. Then I can let myself feel that he doesn't really care."

* * *

Think about each of your family members and friends. Do you care about them, and they about you? Do you feel their opinion of you is accurate? Do you think that they give you enough? Or too much? Do you ever doubt their love or sincerity? Are you open with them, or do you not trust your feelings to them? Do you feel they know you?

Think about the kinds of problems you have with each one. Do any of them smell suspiciously of the twerp's interference?

LOVE AND SEX

Several of the twerp's less sterling qualities come into play in this vital and vulnerable area of our lives.

It gets its two cents' worth in on the ground floor. Look at the pitfalls of first dates. Right off the bat, the twerp makes it hard really to see the new person as a whole, because all it's interested in is isolated details: "Does he have nice hands?" "Would my friends think he's good looking?" "Why does he use that expression?" "I would never have pictured myself going out with a guy who wears a shirt like that." "I wonder how much money he makes."

Then you worry about yourself: "Does he like me?" "Does he think I'm properly dressed?" "Would he be embarrassed to introduce me to his friends?" "I'm not being very entertaining." "Does he think I'm pretty?" "Will he notice that I have a very short neck?"

Then the twerp will make you worry about what to say, and spill your wine, and wonder whether he'll like you in bed. In short, the twerp may be concerned with everything but what's important: What that person is really like and whether you care for him.

Images and expectations are anathema to love and sexual pleasure. The more fixated we are on how things are supposed to be, the less open we are to the range of people we might be interested in, to the diversity of sexual pleasures, to the many ways that a loving relationship can express itself.

"For years, I realize now, I dated the same kind of women over and over. I've always been a sucker for a pretty face, especially for a certain kind of blond, all-American-girl look. When I'd meet a woman who fell into my narrow definition of attractiveness, I'd zoom in on her, take her out, proud of my conquest, proud to be seen with her. Some of these women I'd fall madly in love with, and end up terribly disappointed a few weeks or months later without understanding why.

"The woman I'm with now looks nothing like the women I've dated in the past. I met her through my work—we were thrown together as part of a combined effort of our companies to raise money for the local symphony.

"When I met her, her looks weren't a consideration. It was a business acquaintance, and I wasn't even open to women of her 'type.' When I came to like her so much and to think about dating her, I was shocked to realize that in fact she was very attractive. To this day I look at her and wonder what was wrong with me that I didn't see it.

"In my former dating days, I never expected the women I went out with to be particularly intellectually stimulating or witty or involved in exciting things. In fact, I realize I didn't even expect them to be warm or loving or honorable. And often that's what I'd get—a beautiful woman who knew that her beauty was all I required and who took advantage of it. I guess that's why eventually these relationships broke up."

The sexual arena is fraught with problems. The twerp is a bounder in bed. It has two powerful fixations in this arena— the Organ and the Orgasm. First, your body image: My figure is shapeless, I'm flabby, my tits are too saggy, my cock is too small, I smell, I have too much pubic hair, I have too little pubic hair, my mole is so ugly. The twerp will convince you that you can't have sexual pleasure because looks are everything and *you* have a pimple. The emotional climate for enjoyable sex—trust, arousal, excitement, relaxation, companionability—are destroyed by anxious preoccupation with things that have little to do with pleasure. And if self-confidence and being at ease with your body are prerequisites for good sex, then you must be on guard for the appearance of the critical, fault-finding twerp.

"After I got my divorce, I became obsessed with how my body was aging. I was constantly noticing every little wrinkle and sag, horrified and repelled by the decay, sure that it put me out of the running for sex. I had always been vain about my good figure, and here it was deserting me just when I needed it. When I would be out on a date, all I could think of was how I couldn't take off my clothes because of the repulsive sagging of my arms, or my drooping belly. Sometimes I would be so distracted I'd lose track of my date's conversation. And I'd think of reasons to put off having sex. I guess this was my Inner Enemy's way of keeping me from having sex—of making me feel worse about my divorce, unattractive and unsure of myself. Or maybe it was my guilt about sex."

"I was so convinced that my penis was too small that I went to extraordinary lengths to avoid being seen in the locker room, to avoid any possibility of sex. This was a constant source of torment to me, a constant preoccupation and worry; it's impossible to describe how consumed I was with my problem. It was a woman who "seduced" me the year after I graduated from college—a woman I had come to like and trust, who literally got me drunk, who showed me not only that my penis was perfectly adequate for sex, but that it wasn't so terribly small. And she was right; it's pretty average, in fact. This was an incredible revelation; now I can't even remember where I got the idea that I was so undersized. It seems crazy to me that I spent so many years and so much anguish over this. I'm still haunted by this problem—old patterns are hard to break—but slowly I'm gaining confidence and changing that old broken record about my tiny cock."

The other prong of the twerp's sexual fixation is performance: What a lousy lay you are! You're not free enough. You're too uptight. You don't know all the tricks, all the positions. In bed you feel pressured to prove your virility and experience, your acrobatic endurance; or your cocksucking virtuosity, your fever pitches of excitement. Or perhaps your twerp thinks all that sucking and licking is disgusting.

And what about that orgasm? Are you going to come? How many times? Or what about your erection? Aren't you afraid you won't be able to get it up, or that it won't be hard enough, or that you'll lose it suddenly, or come too fast? This is the classic case of wishing will make it so.

"Sex is always disappointing for me because the only way I can really come is lying on my stomach in a certain position. I've never had the nerve to tell anyone what I like; I'm sure they would think I was strange or perverted and that would be the end of it."

"I can't bring myself to go down on a woman. It just seems filthy to me, not at all pleasurable. So many of the things women like to do in bed seem wrong to me. Lovemaking to me is kissing and hugging and intercourse. I don't enjoy the laughing and tickling and slapping and acrobatics. That's not what sex is about."

These are tough times for sexual pleasure. The offices of psychiatrists and sex therapists are full of people whose sex lives are unsatisfying, whose sexual functioning is impaired.

Impotence and frigidity in the midst of the sexual revolution
are epidemic.

There are countless ways in which the twerp can short-
circuit sexual pleasure. It may have fixed ideas about what is
"right" and what is "wrong." Perhaps it has ideas that have
been passed down from strict parents or a religious upbring-
ing, perhaps magazine- and movie-induced images of what
"great" sex is supposed to be like. The impotent and the
frigid are not the only casualties of the sexual revolution. The
sexually satiated swingers and the jaded playboys also end up
in therapy wondering why they are depressed and dissatisfied, why sex seems so mechanized and detached. People talk
today about the "New Celibacy"—a euphemism for what
happens to people who are disillusioned, burned out by too
much unsatisfying sex. Then there are those who haunt the
singles bars looking for love and settling for sex, a poor, self-
esteem-lowering substitute.

"I've given up on sex. I used to go out all the time—it's
easy for me to get dates, and I used to think it was fun. A little wine, a little grass, and I could go all night. I loved the
feeling of turning guys on—some of them had never met anyone like me, so free and easy. Then all of a sudden I just
stopped getting turned on; no amount of grass or booze
helped. I was just dry as a bone. For a while I just faked it
because I wanted the popularity, wanted the affection, but it
didn't work. I felt exploited by the men I dated. I realized
most of them just wanted the sex; whatever else I got was in
my head. I was angry and was hostile to my dates. Then I got
depressed and had no interest in going out. I'm spending
most of my time by myself now, trying to figure out what I
want. It seems safe to me to avoid sex, and I've lost interest
anyway. One of these days the urge will come back, I suppose."

*   *   *

Then, there's love. Suppose you manage to tame the twerp through the pitfalls of dating and sexual mating, and then you fall in love. The Inner Enemy still has lots of ammunition. First of all, you can fall in love with someone more of the twerp's choosing than of your allies', someone who will have the same growth-stifling, stagnating, critical effects of the twerp. Or you'll set such impossible standards that you will never fall in love. Or the twerp will hinder the transition from the "crazy in love" stage to the realities of a day-to-day relationship, and you'll be furious when the images of romantic love aren't sustained every minute, that the laundry has to get done, furious that your beloved likes rock and roll or has other friends.

"I'd love to settle down and get married. Having children is important to me and I'm almost thirty-six. But I can't seem to find a man I know I'd be happy living with for the rest of my life. I meet and go out with many men. For the first few dates, everything's fine and I really fall for them. But as soon as the novelty wears off, I get bored. They don't seem as interesting to me, and I can see all the things that are wrong, all the reasons why it would be a mistake. Sometimes I've really built the person up, and I'm crushed. I know I'm very fussy, but I'd rather not marry than end up with someone I didn't love and respect."

The twerp may bombard you with doubts about the other person's love and concern, may set up impossible tests to prove that love. The twerp will remind you of how unworthy you are of the love you've found; it will make you do things that prove you're unlovable. Because you're afraid that in an intimate relationship you'll be revealed as an imposter, your twerp will cause you to back off, to create a barrier, a safety zone, between you and your beloved, much to your lover's confusion and dismay.

The twerp feels that being so happily in love is too good for the likes of you and will do what it can to sabotage it. A woman may unconsciously feel so undeserving of the wonderful lover she's found that she cheats on him and goes out with another man. She does this partially to prove to herself she's unworthy of the man who loves her, half hoping (and yet fearing) that he will find out and know what a terrible person she is. A man who can't believe that he is loved may find fault with his loving woman—to bring her down in his eyes to where he can believe she is capable of being in love with him, to temper his joy so as not to make trouble, to give him an excuse not to be so much in love.

How about you? Do you have very particular ideas about the people you date? Where did you get these ideas? Or do you date many different types of people? Do you feel you choose your dates well; i.e., do you usually enjoy their company? Do they have the qualities you admire? Or are you often disappointed, find they don't measure up to your expectations?

Do you feel limited in your choice of dates—do you consider some people "too good for you," others "beneath you"?

What are you interested in when you first go out with someone? Are you curious about that person? Curious about how he or she feels about you? Are you critical of that person? How many dates do you usually have with each one? Do you worry about whether you'll see each person again? What does your twerp think of your dates? Or your attractiveness to them?

And sex? Do you feel self-conscious about your body or about any particular physical flaws? Does it interfere with your enjoyment of sex or your decision to have sex with a new partner? Is sex fun for you, or do you feel too much pressure to have great sex? Do you feel you're good at it? Do you know what turns you on? Are you able to express your preferences and get satisfaction? Are there things that turn you off or that you feel are wrong? Do you have sex frequently enough? Or too often? Do you ever find yourself in bed with someone, unable to get turned on? Or do you sometimes lose interest in the middle of things? Do you know why?

What happens when you fall in love? Do you do so easily? Do you fall in love with people who are supportive and good to you? Does the love last? If not, what happens? Do you become disillusioned or disappointed in your beloved? Why do you think this is? What happens when the romantic glow fades? Are you able to keep the love alive while adjusting to the realities of everyday life? Do you feel confident of the other person's love? Are you afraid that love will fade or cease? Do you feel you've fooled your beloved, that you'll be found out? Do you ever test the love of others? How? What happens? Are you ever critical of those you love? How? Do you feel relieved when you find flaws? Are your relationships balanced? Or do you feel that you have to do "more" to deserve the love you get? Or that you're entitled to take it easy?

TWERP TIMING: THE INNER ENEMY IN CRISIS AND CONFLICT

Across the board, in whatever arena the twerp is active, it is sure to speak up more vociferously in times of conflict or crisis. For these times herald potential change, growth, newness. And the twerp is always anxious about change.

We humans are by nature problem solving. Conflicts of whatever magnitude offer us the opportunity for learning and growth; and the twerp is not always happy to see us making decisions, overcoming difficulties:

"I have a bad habit of not facing up to unpleasant situations, especially when they involve personal confrontations. For weeks I'd been agonizing over a situation with a woman friend who is also a partner in a small business venture with me. My feeling was that I was doing too much of the work, and that our original agreement had to be revised. I also had reservations about the way she was approaching new customers. For weeks I stewed about the situation—rationalizing that it wasn't really so bad, that I was wrong, thinking it would work out by itself. Finally, I took the grown-up step and called her and had a long conversation in which we discussed all these upsetting matters. I felt that the conversation went well and that I handled myself very well. When I got off the phone I was proud of myself, and sat there for a moment basking in the glow of my accomplishment, dimly aware of the little voice in the background saying, 'So big deal. You made a phone call. You should have done it weeks ago.' Then I got up to go make a cup of tea, tripped over my typewriter table and took a very bad spill. My successful call was evidently more than my Inner Enemy could handle."

Every person makes a series of decisions, large and small, every day of his life. The importance of being able to handle decisions is magnified in these times of great freedom of action and choice. Weighing information, reviewing options, we make choices about everything from when to get up, what to wear, how long to spend reading the paper, what to have for breakfast, to important things like what kind of career to pursue, whom to fall in love with, whether to have children.[4]

The twerp has many ways to foul up this vital process. It will throw in so much information, so many conflicting opinions that making a choice becomes difficult or impossible. It will make us fearful of the change inherent in decisions so that we avoid them, put them off, or choose the safest alter-

4. For a thorough study of the decision-making process, consult Harold Greenwald's book, listed in the Bibliography.

native. We become decision-phobic, unable to know what we want or what is best. When this happens, *nothing* happens. We stagnate and can't move forward. Sometimes the decision-making process becomes so stressful that we have a hard time deciding *anything*—even what kind of sandwich we want for lunch.

The weight of the twerp's opinion must be monitored in crisis because it has a tendency to cut down on objectivity, to use its veto power to override positive innovative suggestions: The Inner Enemy is a doubting Thomas all the way. Sometimes it takes over unauthorized duties, and sabotages order and fair debate and the decision-making process. Also, being ignorant and fearful of context, it lacks integrative perspective and fixates on simple-minded, safe solutions. The twerp is uncomfortable with the complexity involved in making a decision. It will rule out nuances of thought in favor of making a clear-cut choice, of avoiding ambiguity. And in doing so, it cuts down on our options. If the Inner Enemy's voice is too loud and cuts in too often, it will become the tie breaker that makes the important decisions affecting the course of our lives.

The best defense against the twerp's interference is to be aware of the predictable crisis and conflict situations in which it is bound to show up: When you're meeting new people or falling in love, when you're ill, when good fortune strikes unexpectedly, *when you're contemplating any kind of change.* You can anticipate that the twerp will surface in any decision-making situation, especially if the decision involves self-realization—a new job, a career change, a decision to hire part-time help to take care of the kids so you can have some free time.

Having the twerp around at decision time is not always all bad. In the area of problem solving, of weighing possibilities, it can provide a cautious, historical voice, reminding us of what's gone before. The problem is, that's all it knows, and its advice comes from sources that are often negative or discredited. It's still making the decision that was most judicious when you were in fourth grade. Here's an example of how the twerp's interference in one situation served as a lesson for what could have been a much more serious disaster:

"I met my girlfriend in midtown Manhattan near my office at lunchtime one day to do some shopping for my house. As we walked across Fifty-seventh Street, I stopped to watch a game of three-card monte that had a small crowd gathered around it. This game is similar to the old shell game: The object is to identify the position of one of three cards after the dealer has shuffled them around very quickly—talking all the time—on a small table. Now, this is a notorious scam—these fast-talking dealers have shills in the crowd to keep the action going; huge amounts of money change hands. It's as phony as a three-dollar bill.

"Anyway, before I knew it, I was betting $50, $150, on this game. When I'd lose, the shill in the crowd would suddenly win a round. Then they'd offer me a bonus—a free try to play again. My girlfriend couldn't believe I was doing it. After the third bet—I'd probably dropped $150—she dragged me away. It was like I'd been in a trance; I didn't realize what I was doing. It was so unlike me, so out of character, that it was spooky. Not only am I not a gambler, but I hate these crooks; I don't even like the street peddlers that clutter the streets of midtown.

"The only explanation I have for this bizarre behavior is that the twerp was trying to teach me something. Right before I left for lunch a friend had called me with a very hot 'rumor' about a company merger—which would have the effect of driving the stock price way up a few days later. Now, this kind of thing, trading on what may have been inside information, is illegal, and it's certainly off limits for someone in my business. Yet as I left the office, I was very tempted to use that information and make the very tidy quick profit it would afford. In playing and losing at three-card monte, I think the twerp was telling me very clearly not to get involved in this shady get-rich-quick scheme. As if to drive the message home, on the way back from our shopping, we passed the 'scene of the crime'—the game—just as three plainclothes cops were arresting and handcuffing the guys."

The inner debate below, recorded by Marcia while she was taking Dr. Bach's Inner Enemy course, demonstrates the complexity of conflicting opinions, of opposing voices, that can make decision making so difficult. Yet hearing out the voices is imperative, for the decision should be made with the participation of all parties; no one voice should be allowed to outshout the others.

Sunday night, about 8:30. Neal Barren from New York calls. He and Arthur are in town. Both young, bright, high-rolling, lovely men, have a film distribution company. Here in LA to do business, staying at the Beverly Wilshire. Asked me to come over tonight, have a drink with them, room 510, they have Jim Beam, tequila, and good grass. I really could go. My son is away. No early morning appointments.

RECLUSE: Stay home, Marcia. Organize your income-tax data for your accountant tomorrow. Get it all out of the way so tomorrow morning at five you can get back to your writing.

MARCIA: OK. That's what I'll do. But isn't it lovely of them to want me? They're both superattractive, superbright. They must like me. Neal made me feel delicious on the phone. I laughed and gurgled with pleasure.

GERMAN GOVERNESS: They've been in town two and a half weeks, he said. Why didn't they call you sooner? If you go and have pot and drink and sex with them, you'll be an easy lay. Not good for future business with them. Besides two against one. They could beat you up, wipe you out, and no one would know where you are. Do you know, absolutely *know*, that they're not kinky and like to beat up women? Stay away. Don't be a fool, Marcia.

MARCIA: You're right. I hate your skepticism but I'm staying home.

PARTY GIRL STAR: Goddam you, Marcia. Oh God, I'm so sad. You never let me play. You keep me shut in all the time. I'm going to die and you'll be sorry. It would be yummy to get high with them. Two sibling figures like the old days with Joe and Kelly in the nursery, giggly and silly. Two loving young men, perfect. You love that combination and have fun. For Christ's sake, let your hair down. You've only one life. TRUST THEM! Jeremy said very few men actually do beat up women. And it doesn't matter at all what they think of you. Take the fruits that are offered. I'm hungry Marcia. You're starving me. It's not fair. I can't live like this.

MARCIA: I'm sorry. I'm really sorry. I'd like to go, too, and see those boys and have fun. But I don't feel I can afford the effort. The time, the output of energy, the cigarette smoke, the risk of other discomforts, the risk of something terrible happening like getting beat up or humiliated, although I myself no longer believe that would happen.

RECLUSE: Don't betray me, Marcia. Get that bullshit account stuff done tonight so tomorrow morning you can get back to the writing. You have a radio interview to prepare. You have a magazine article to write. You have two books to finish.

MARCIA: I'm crying now because it's been two months since Peter. Two months since I've had a man's arms around me. I'm lonely and hungry to be touched.

PARTY GIRL STAR: Go to the Wilshire. To the Wilshire. The checkbook can wait. The books can wait. The article can wait. You need a hypodermic of joy-juice.

MARCIA: Stop that! Stop tempting me. I don't need any such damn thing! I won't be distracted! I won't coddle myself! I do not need to screw around tonight with two light guys, two transient playboy businessmen, young and all that, but decidedly transient. Decidedly passers-by. They've been here two weeks and didn't call me. They're leaving tomorrow or the next day. Now what does that mean? Certainly not lasting friendship or love!

PARTY GIRL STAR: *Nothing* lasts, dummy, nothing. You're trying to buy immortality with your book and that won't work. Nothing lasts! It's all leaves in autumn. You're chasing a mirage.

RECLUSE: I'm not saying anything. I have nothing to say. The fight is between you two. Marcia and I have a clear conscience.

MARCIA: Yes. Clear. And I'm afraid I'd get drunk and high and be unable to drive home. But on the other hand it makes me kind of sick to look at that business-size envelope with my accountant's check and notes in it. Do I want to live like him? No. Do I want to vote for that way of life? No.

Recluse: Too many distractions. You don't need fun. You don't need to be touched. You need peace and quiet. *Less* touching. *Less* fun. *Fewer* interruptions. You had a lovely evening with Carl Parks last night. That suffices. You had a beautiful evening with Rich on Tuesday. Two evenings with men in one week. That's ample.

Marcia: But they weren't sexual.

Recluse: No? Masturbating over the phone isn't sexual? Talking with Carl about the test he's devising to measure sexual interest—that's not sexual?

Marcia: That's talking about sex. That's not direct sex.

Recluse: It's sexual. And you've masturbated this week a lot more times than in a long time. Isn't that sexual?

Marcia: Yes. But alone.

Recluse: What were your thoughts when you masturbated?

Marcia: I thought of a man making love to me who loves me. Possibly Rich, sometimes Rich, saying he loves me. I thought of going to San Francisco and seeing him for dinner, staying in his apartment, arguing about not staying in his apartment, making love to him, he's very persistent, he likes to screw a lot, that's my fantasy. That's what I thought about when I masturbated.

Recluse: It's clear then that you do not fantasize about two young, light-hearted, light-mouthed, light-cocked men who ask you at the last minute to come drink and smoke with them and whatever at the Wil-

shire. You fantasize about one man loving you passion-
ately. One man you love. One man.

MARCIA: Yes. It's clear. Party Girl Star, my longing
for the Wilshire comes from a bad dream. I talked on
the phone with Peter recently and felt no sexual excitement at all. That gypsy carpenter romance is dead. The
transient sex and pot in a hotel bedroom are dead. All I
can think of is the cigarette smoke and how will I drive
myself home.

PARTY GIRL STAR: OK. You win this time. But I'm
warning you. You've got to find a way to let me out, let
me play. You've won this round. Go do your goddam
desk work. You've won this round, but the battle isn't
over. We're still at war.

MARCIA: I'll remember that and honor it. For now
though, it's armistice.

PARTY GIRL STAR: For now. For this evening. That's
all.

TWERP ALERT REPORT

The purpose of the Twerp Alert Report is to itemize
those situations when the twerp shows up and to articulate
just how it behaves so that we can recognize its arrival and be
prepared to deal with it. As long as it shows up unawares, and
is able to make trouble for a while before we spot it, we're at
its mercy. Filling out the Twerp Alert Report is like drawing
a map of its whereabouts.

Go back over Chapters 7 and 8, in which you itemized
and described the twerp voices; review this chapter and the
questions you just answered, and go through your journals.
These contain all the evidence you have accumulated on the
twerp's behavior. It's time now to evaluate the data, to pick

out the repetitions and redundancies, to make concrete statements about your twerp and draw conclusions. You will be able to figure out what conditions favor twerp activity, and see which arenas it's most active in. You will spot its characteristic behavior, its typical words and catchphrases, its entrance cues.

Itemize as many of them as you can in this report. Then you will have a dossier on the twerp that will tell you exactly what to expect and when. You will sabotage its first-strike capacity.

In filling out your report, make your statements as specific as possible, supported by the evidence you have accumulated, and make as many statements as possible. The suggested categories will help organize your thoughts.

Here are some examples of the kind of information that might appear in a Twerp Alert Report:

"The twerp rarely questions my friendships—certainly not the quality of my friends or their loyalty. When it does, it says, 'Who are you to deserve all these wonderful friends? They must not know the real you.'"

"When I'm with a woman I don't have a deep interest in, I'm fine. If I like her I push her to tell me about her sexual and romantic past, comparing and judging myself—and her. I spoil it."

"Sometimes when I'm really enjoying myself, with friends, even at work, I'll suddenly stop short and a feeling of dread—a physical sensation like chills up my spine—will come over me momentarily. It's the spoiler not wanting me to enjoy myself too much. Usually this feeling is hard to shake."

"Whenever a deadline is really pressing, you can be sure I'll find a dozen small things that must be done first—the laundry, a phone call, an errand, a note, a chore I've been postponing for weeks."

"My procrastinator is pretty blunt. I just sit at my desk all day not getting any work done, staring at the typewriter with butterflies in my stomach. And I won't permit myself to escape it by going out and enjoying myself—as long as I'm not working anyway."

"I recognize my twerp because it says, 'That won't work' in a very convincing tone every time I have an idea."

"I get in late every morning even though I spend every moment from the time I wake thinking about getting in on time."

"Lately my twerp has me completely forgetting business appointments."

"At least five times a day I say to myself, 'I *should* be moving ahead faster in this company,' or 'I *should* be doing more important work at this stage of my life.'"

"The breakup of my marriage—the fights, the reconciliations, the pain—goes around and around in my head constantly, interspersed with me saying, 'What did I do wrong? What could I have done to change it?' I can't ever seem to stop it."

TWERP ALERT REPORT

Where the Twerp Shows Up:	Often	Occasionally	Rarely	Never
Body Image				
Self-care				
Work				
Leisure/Play				
Friends				
Family				
Sex				
Love				

Elaborate each instance: _____

_____

_____

_____

When the Twerp Shows Up:	Often	Occasionally	Rarely	Never
Good Times				
Bad Times				
Decision				
Crisis				
Competition				
Change				

Elaborate what it says: _____
_____
_____
_____

Elaborate what it does: _____
_____
_____
_____

HOW TO FIGHT FAIR
WITH YOURSELF

10

Twerp Access: Ways and Means to Understanding the Inner Dialogue

EVERYONE IS ENTITLED to an inner life. Everyone should be able to enjoy the riches of the imagination, of complexity and paradox. The pleasure of one's own company can be wonderful; at the very least it's an antidote to loneliness. But although most people recognize the existence of the Inner Enemy and acknowledge its powerful hold on their lives, they often come up empty-handed when they try to tune in and find out what it's up to. Some people are too busy to go chasing after the twerp. They don't pay attention to what's going on in there, or they listen halfheartedly—and half fearfully—and are discouraged by the seemingly impenetrable babble. Or they are so closed off from their inner lives that they cannot decipher the twerp's message. They have no time to ruminate, to brood, to wonder, to ponder. They are out of touch with what is happening inside, and defensive against what they feel is a threatening assault on their carefully constructed existence.

Habits of negligence, of defense or denial, are difficult to change. But it can be done. Slowly, safely, in small steps, by building new habits, opening new channels, developing new skills, and setting aside time, the twerp can be encouraged to show itself.

The techniques outlined here are presented as means of approaching the Inner Enemy and our allies—via the Inner Dialogue. They are all ways to find out what's going on in there, and all can enrich our inner lives.

THE WALK/TALK

Walking has long been touted as excellent all-around physical exercise. But walking is also mentally and emotionally therapeutic. Dr. Bach discovered the benefits of the Walk/Talk during his years of practice in Hollywood.

He found that patients who were "stuck" in therapy were often moved to talk much more easily if he and the patient spent their therapy session in a leisurely stroll through the local park. The very act of moving seemed to get the mental and emotional processes going. Other factors seem to weigh into why the Walk/Talk is so liberating. It turns inner drive into outer knowledge and information. Walking and looking around take the inhibiting or confrontational quality out of trying to force out talk and insight. The pressure is removed, our attention is sidetracked, defenses fall a bit. It takes our mind off the job. Also, the longer we walk the more our unconscious takes over; we go into a kind of overdrive.

Taking a Walk/Talk with yourself is a pleasant and painless way to get a handle on the Inner Enemy. You can be sure it will come along. It is not necessary to have a specific goal for a Walk/Talk—nothing more is required than a desire to take the time and see what happens. As the feet wander, let the mind wander. Don't be afraid to talk aloud to yourself— it is no longer considered lunatic behavior.

Use the walk to think about what has happened during

the day, to remember the people you have seen or spoken to, the work you have done, the pleasures or problems that have come up. Even seemingly trivial thoughts like what you ate for breakfast or the color of the flowers are fine.

See what happens, if any voices pipe up or if you get off on a particular train of thought—examining a particular problem, daydreaming about some person in your life. If one of your voices speaks up, if a dialogue gets started, encourage it. Interview your voices, visit with them, listen to them, befriend them. Allow them to speak.

The Walk/Talk is one of the very best ways for making contact with the enemy—or with your allies. Set aside a bit of time each day for this walk—the longer the better, but even a stroll around the block or around the yard a few times is helpful. As you build the habit of Walk/Talking, the dialogue will become more open and easy, will add a richness to your life and a sense of inner union and wholeness, despite the many voices that have something to say.

Imagine yourself with different companions on a Walk/Talk. Use what you've learned about your Inner Enemy to identify the parties to the dialogue. Visit with each of your voices—allies and enemies: today the Spoiler, tomorrow the Fan. Find out what they're up to. Have them talk to each other. Make deals with them; negotiate for change or better behavior. Learn to be a competent communicator. You can even take a Walk/Talk with an invisible friend, with a historical figure such as Freud or Babe Ruth. Take a Walk/Talk with an idea—creativity, weather, progress, power. You can pose a problem: Should I accept that raise or ask for more money? How can I stop myself from drinking at the next office party? Should I have another baby? Once you make a habit of the Walk/Talk and become receptive to its benefits, it will all come out in the walk.

SLOW-MOTION REPLAY

One of the hardest tasks in trying to unravel the Inner Dialogue is capturing what goes on—the voices speak so fast and they all talk at once. They have difficult idioms and speech patterns. It can be very helpful if when you are fortunate enough to be able to grab a bit of the dialogue—even if it's only a phrase or a short exchange—you can slow it down and repeat it to see what you can learn.

It's the same as instant replay on television. In a complex, fast-moving game, one of the several cameras has focused on a small piece of the action, which turns out to be important. So the station shows it again for the viewer's benefit, slowed down so that the viewer can see in detail just how a complicated play was run, or a pass caught, or a crucial exchange of tennis volleys made. The announcer may clarify the event with narration: "Here we see Borg hit a sharp cross-court which forces Connors off-balance in his forehand corner, giving Borg the chance to come in on his weak return for a sharp-angled volley to Conners' backhand. Still reeling from the previous shot, there's no way he can get there in time."

Focus in on the bit of dialogue you were able to isolate and the circumstances under which it occurred, and try to repeat it slowly and clearly:

"I am in the elevator coming down from the Registration Office at the New School, where I just signed up for a course on current archaeological digs. I am excited but a bit nervous that I won't have as much background as the other students and will be way behind and seem stupid. As the elevator door opens I realize that again today I didn't call my friend Susan. I chastise myself for this. As I step off I remember that yesterday was Larry's birthday and I forgot to send him a card. I feel awful. Suddenly I remember very clearly a whole list of people whom I haven't kept up with or haven't seen lately.

In a crystal-clear voice I hear Arlene complaining that she can never pin me down to go to a movie. I feel very hot and claustrophobic as I push open the door, and I think about how upset with me Alison seemed last time I saw her and I wondered then if she liked me. When I stepped outside, I broke into a big smile because I was so happy I'd finally signed up for an archaeology course."

Replay this dialogue as many times as you need to in order to see it clearly in as much detail as possible. Who was talking? What provoked the exchange? Was it a fair debate? Have you heard this one before? Who won? Try and draw conclusions from the replay that will help you contend with the twerp in the future.

Here is Fran's analysis:

"I was excited about taking the course, even though I'm a bit afraid that I won't be able to keep up. I felt good that I'd finally signed up—good that I mustered the nerve to overcome my apprehensions, good that I'd set aside time in a busy schedule. But as soon as I started to congratulate myself, the voices of guilt and responsibility and a Spoiler showed up. They wanted to remind me of how I had neglected my friends, point out how selfish I am, threaten me with the loss of my friends, make me feel bad, or reconsider what I was doing. I realize that in fact I am probably *overly* conscientious about my friends, and that sometimes I use what I consider my duty to them to postpone doing other things, especially things for myself. As I replay this dialogue, I realize that the same conversation has occurred in various forms many times before, most often when I want to do something for myself—especially if it involves trying something new. The twerp never directly says no, but I realize now that I use my friends quite often as a front for keeping me from exploring new things. I have to be aware of this in the future."

* * *

Another way to use the instant-replay technique is to focus in on something that happened recently when it seemed the twerp was at work: an unpleasant exchange with your spouse or child, something that went wrong at work, a mistake, a personal failure, a fight with a friend, a poor decision. Replay the incident in your mind and see if focusing in on the dynamics of it brings the twerp to the surface. It may speak up while you are reliving the experience and help you shed some light on what happened. You will have even more clues about how the twerp works in certain situations, and you will know better how to cope with it if a similar situation arises in the future.

DAYDREAMS

In our high-powered culture, daydreaming is considered a frivolous waste of time. In fact, daydreaming can be extremely useful and productive. Many great artists and scientists have reported that inspiration came not while they had their nose to the grindstone but as a result of staring out the window daydreaming when they "should have been working." Daydreaming allows us to explore our wishes and longings, gives us insight into our hopes and dreams. It gives us leisure to consider various options, to peruse hypothetical situations, to come up with creative imaginative scenarios without being burdened with the practical logistics and considerations that at other times might cause us to abandon our dreams too easily.

Setting aside time to daydream and paying attention to the messages in those dreams serve two main functions in dealing with the Inner Enemy. First, daydreaming will flush the twerp out of hiding, because it will surely have something to say when you want to abandon yourself to such frivolity.

Second—and more important—daydreaming is an easy and pleasant way to explore aspirations and longings that the twerp would rather you didn't think about. It will put you more in touch with the person you wish to be.

There are two steps to the daydream technique. One is to set aside time to do it. It is all too easy never to have a moment to be able to sit still, to think and reflect. The Inner Enemy loves this, because it figures you will just spin your wheels a lot if you don't have time for plans and strategy. So set aside just two or three minutes a couple of times a day— and tell yourself very specifically that it's for daydreaming.

Second, plan your daydreaming. Most of the time you will just want to let your mind wander and think of wonderful things—places to go, things to do, people to meet. But it is possible to daydream about the things that concern you at the moment. If you are dissatisfied with your work or planning a career change, daydream about the perfect job and think about all your skills and the things you know how to do. Try to imagine yourself working in a place you love. If you have been fighting with your spouse, imagine the situation in which she (or he) understands you and is loving toward you. Imagine the most beautiful place to live when you are trying to decide where to move and to what kind of house. Imagine the most delicious meal whenever you can't figure out what you want for lunch. Even simple issues can be approached in daydreams.

Sally knew that she was very timid about fashion and could never tell what looked good on her. She tended to wear very basic things, the kind of clothes that everyone wore. She always looked nice. She had a good figure and a good color sense. But she never felt right in her clothes and never knew quite what to do about it. Then one day when she was feeling particularly drab and unexciting, she started daydreaming about herself in all kinds of clothes and colors and costumes unlike any she had ever worn before. She saw very clear images of herself not in ridiculous costumes or high-fashion designs, but pretty, flattering clothes—outfits that she had seen many times before in fashion layouts, or on other people, but had never thought about wearing. But somewhere inside, Sally had a clear picture of how she would like to look and what would look well on her. When she allowed herself to daydream, some of these ideas surfaced. Sally has since changed her style of dressing considerably and feels "more herself" in her new clothes and likes the way she looks. Now she uses the daydream technique not only to conjure up her new wardrobe, but to learn other things about herself as well.

TWERP HEYDAY

In a way the Twerp Heyday technique is similar to daydreaming—but the result is more like a bad dream. In using this technique, we give the Inner Enemy free rein and allow it to say and do whatever it wants, to go as far as it wants, to be outrageous and overbearing. Every dog will have its day, as the saying goes, and this one belongs to the twerp.

There are good reasons for letting the twerp run loose. First of all, we see the range and scope, the full bizarre panorama, of its activities so that we become aware of even its more peripheral manifestations. More important, by actively encouraging what appears to be a twerp takeover, we realize that we do have some contol, even in this seemingly twerp-dominated situation. We learn that even at its worst, the Inner Enemy can be stood up to, laughed at, baited, talked back to. We can see, especially in this overblown situation, just what a blowhard it can be.

This exercise is based on the assumption that if you give the twerp enough rope, it will hang itself. Also, the Twerp

Heyday exercise employs some of the twerp's own tricks. This is the way to go about it: Choose a time when you feel strong enough to let the Inner Enemy run amok—not when you are trying to make a crucial decision or feeling overextended or fragile. Then when the twerp shows up, instead of ignoring it or denying it's there, try to bait it, to draw it out. You can trick it into thinking it's overpowering you. Act dominated. Pretend to agree with what it says, go along with its opinion. Pretend you're giving in. If the twerp likes to browbeat you about your looks while you're putting on your makeup, pretend to go along. Encourage even more outrageous comments. Add some of your own: "You think my eyes are too close together? Well, what about this mousy hair? And you call this a hairstyle? And wait till you see the ridiculous blouse I'm going to wear."

If you tend to drink too much at parties and then say things you don't mean, tell yourself, and your twerp, that you are going to drink even more than usual and that you will say something really insulting.

If your pattern is to make yourself sick when you are under pressure (or when things are going well), do it. Plan on getting sick, think about it, look for symptoms everywhere, revel in it.

If your twerp has a favorite broken record, don't try and stop it next time. Play it over and over and over; see if you can find new refrains to add to it.

An artist who has had his share of creative-block problems reports:

"I had had one of those all-too-infrequent mornings when I worked intensely, absorbedly, feverishly in my studio, untroubled by the usual thoughts and doubts. When I finally paused a moment—I realized I was hungry and had to go to the bathroom—I had a feeling of real accomplishment and happiness at those old juices flowing. I set off for the kitchen full of ideas for the afternoon . . . for the whole week's work.

"Well, it was a joke. First, I spilled turpentine and had to waste fifteen minutes cleaning it up. Then I tripped over a light cord. I dropped my mail. I couldn't remember a phone number I had known for years. Couldn't get the top off a bottle. Fortunately I recognized the twerp at work and since I was in a good mood—and it seemed determined to provoke me and undo all the good feelings of the morning—I decided to lead it on. I talked out loud to it as I went about my business. 'OK, maybe I'll dial the wrong number when I call Amy. She probably doesn't care if I call anyway. I think I'll spill my soup. Ooops! Look! Almost a disaster. Let's see if I can cut my finger on this can. I think I'll knock over my vitamins. I'm awfully clumsy. And that really wasn't such great stuff I did this morning. I think I'll go back to the studio and paint it all out. Maybe get paint on my clothes!'

"This worked, miraculously. The twerp seemed to be eating it up. I kept thinking of more and more devastating things to say. I really learned something about how my twerp operated: It didn't undermine my work—it undermined the *rest* of my life, and kept me from getting back to work. Now I recognize this pattern and cope with it better; I don't get so easily sidetracked and don't feel so weakened by these bouts of ineptitude. Now that I can laugh at this infantile twerp behavior, it happens less often and I can often cut the length of the twerp's visit. Certainly its impact is no longer so devastating."

Twerp Heyday can be likened to an exorcism in that by being let loose, the twerp burns itself out. By laughing at it— "You've got to be kidding," "You make me sick"—you open a festering sore and let the malignant, infectious invective run out.

This may seem silly or dangerous, but in fact it will demonstrate that when you are aware of the twerp and are braced for its onslaught, it loses much of its power to hurt and devastate you—even in its most wildly outrageous form. In fact, the twerp, looked at this way, begins to seem ludicrous; it becomes easier to dismiss and discount its criticisms, easier to talk back to it, easier to avoid its traps. Giving the devil his due is a good idea in this instance. The twerp will try and have its way with or without your permission, with or without your controlling influence. It's in your best interest to be as active a participant as possible when it decides to run wild.

You've heard of mind control? Twerp Heyday is the opposite: mind abandon. We loosen our fearful, fretful hold on what's happening inside and let it run free. And what we feared would be a gruesome, irrational monster often turns out to be the twerp making a fool of itself.

DREAMS

Dreams are a rich source of information about the Inner Enemy and about inner allies. Dreams always tell the truth, they are creative, they are about waking issues and concerns. There is only one problem: Most people have a hard time remembering them. Or they can remember them only fleetingly, or can recall only a small cameo from a larger dream. The twerp censors dreams unmercifully; it doesn't want to be found out, doesn't want to see problems grappled with and solved.

Even when dreams are remembered, they are often puzzling, seemingly nonsensical. They appear weird, even frightening, filled with symbols and allusions that make no sense in one's waking life.

The importance of dreams has perhaps been overempha-

sized by a psychiatric community still closely tied to rigid
Freudian ideas. Many lay people are loath to take seriously
the import attributed to dreams, the fixed meanings attributed to the symbols in them. They find it hard to accept that
lilies always mean innocence, a hallway is the vagina, a pole
is the phallus, that certain numbers and colors have prede-
termined significance. It's too much mumbo jumbo, especially when the symbolic meaning doesn't make sense in the
context of their lives.

What is called for is a less pedantic, more personalized,
lighthearted approach to dreams. Dreams are personal, idio-
syncratic creations—only the individual can interpret their
meaning with real expertise. Also, they can be a source of
interest and entertainment. At best, they are a tool for exploring ideas and solving problems to which we bring those
unconscious resources not available in our waking lives.
Dreams give us a broader palette to work with.

Everyone's ability to tune in to and remember his dreams
differs. There are people who never remember dreams or remember them rarely, momentarily, or in fragments. There
are those who on occasion remember an entire dream clearly.
Some people remember all their dreams and can recount
three or ten stories every morning. Some have lucid dreams,
in which they are "awake" and aware of dreaming; sometimes these people can forcibly alter the course of their
dreams.

We cannot simply will ourselves to remember dreams, for
the censoring conscience won't make it that easy. And it is
not likely that habits of a lifetime will change overnight and
we will suddenly wake up with full-blown Technicolor
dreams to report. However, we can try to chip away at the
barriers surrounding our dreams by understanding that the
twerp doesn't want us to have the benefits of our dreams, and
by becoming less fearful of the twerp's power. The Inner
Enemy would like us to believe that we have something to

fear from our weird, puzzling dreams, when what we really have to fear is the twerp and our own ignorance of what the dreams mean. All dreams are strange and weird if judged by standards of the real world; but everything that happens in dreams is OK and is not to be feared. So we must ally ourselves with the part of us that wants to grow and enjoy ourselves, understanding that our dreams can help us be more creative and whole.

Before you go to sleep, remind yourself that you are going to dream and that you would like to remember your dreams. Then upon waking, don't move around or speak or start thinking of your day. Lie very still and see whether there isn't some residue from your last dream. This is about all you can do, and results may not be immediately forthcoming. However, if you do this every night in good faith, or as you become more familiar with your twerp and more confident that you can handle it, the likelihood is that you will remember a bit of a dream, and then a little more, with increasing frequency.

What then? Write the dream down: It is an elusive creature. And what are you to make of it? Well, that's the point: It's entirely up to you. It's your dream, your own creation. The dream has whatever importance you want to attach to it, and in the end, only you can determine its meaning. It may help to know basic symbol interpretations, but chances are that if a hallway or the number thirteen appears in a dream, it has a more direct and personal meaning for you than the textbook interpretation. Once you have written down your dream, see if there is an immediate meaning that is clear to you:

"I probably dreamed about watching a baseball game because tonight is my first date with Herb and he likes sports. I was trying very hard to follow the game though I didn't understand it—the sequence of events, the field, the uniforms, made no sense to me. Again, I think this is because I am curious about Herb, and I know very little about him." Perhaps you are able to figure out the meaning of the dream as a whole in the context of your waking life. If not, you must look at each of the components.

The next step is to break the dream down into little pieces, for there is no waste—everything counts, every little image means something, even if it's hard to figure out. Who was in the dream (it's interesting to note that we are rarely alone in dreams; dreams recognize our social nature)? Where did it take place? What was in the room or landscape? What clothes were worn? Were any colors, or numbers, prominent? What was said? Any special phrases used? When did it happen? How much time passed? What was the mood of the dreams? What actions took place?

What does each of these elements mean? That is up to you. Look at each piece separately and see what reaction you have, what associations you can make to it. Let your imagination go. Be creative and freehanded with your interpretations and speculations. Think of the wildest explanation, several explanations, fanciful and serious explanations:

"The number thirteen could be bad luck. Or it's one more than a dozen—so I'm a leftover; or it's one and three—the lottery numbers. Or it's thirteen weeks in a trimester. Or Channel 13."

Don't strain too hard. If nothing comes to mind it's not terribly important. And if an interpretation is right, you will feel it and trust it.

Not every dream is fraught with significance. Here is Lenore's story:

"I woke up one night and realized that I had had a dream in which I discovered the meaning of life. I was groggy with sleep but determined not to let my portentous dream slip by. So I fumbled for the pen and paper I keep on my night table, scribbled down my dream, and promptly fell back to sleep.

As soon as I woke up the next morning I remembered my dream of the night before and grabbed the pad off the night table, quivering with anticipation about its revelations. The meaning of life! Hot damn! Scrawled across the pad was the following legend: 'Twinkle, twinkle, little star, How I wonder what you are!' "

Lenore could decipher little meaning from her "profound" dream. She hadn't thought of that nursery rhyme in years, or been particularly preoccupied with questions about life's goals or meaning. Perhaps her dream was merely a reminder not to take life—or her dreams—too seriously.

Some researchers believe that in dreams we are just processing the events of the day so we can free our minds of them, like so much garbage. Another theory holds that in our dreams we resolve waking conflicts and therefore sleep through them. Thus, under normal circumstances only unsolvable dream puzzles wake us and are remembered.[5]

Following is a series of dreams recorded by Beatrice while she was taking Dr. Bach's Inner Enemy course at UCLA. Each dream by itself is not particularly exotic or significant. Each reorganizes and reinterprets the incidents and information of daily life. When the dreams are looked at together, however, a pattern emerges. Beatrice was concerned about her career, about the amount of time she devoted to it, its importance to her, its effect on her life-style and family. Recognizing her concern and ambivalence about her work, seeing clearly in her dreams the messages of both inner allies and enemies, Beatrice made it a point to force her attentions on this issue and reach some resolution about it. Here are brief descriptions of her dreams and her capsulized interpretations of them:

5. Montague Ullman and Nan Zimmerman, *Working with Dreams* (New York: Delacorte Press/Eleanor Friede, 1979).

Dream: "I was called by the store manager of our local IGA supermarket and asked if I would like to work part time at the store. I remember thinking that I would probably not like the work but perhaps I *should* take it because I would be earning more money. But I had guests coming, so it would be additionally difficult to entertain a houseful of people and add a new job (to the work I already do). Dream ends with ambivalent feelings about taking the supermarket job."

Interpretation: "The night before I had talked with one of our guests (lots of old friends coming to Santa Monica for the fiftieth anniversary of the Modern Language Department). His wife had just started to work full time and I had a pang of guilt. 'How come I can only manage part-time work?'"

Dream: "We (my children and I) were going on a picnic. We drove across a high bridge, and there was a kind of descending ramp off the side of the bridge into a picnic area below. The trees in the picnic area were very surrealistic in character—all made from feathers instead of leaves. One tree in particular interested me. Its branches were perfectly sculptured—and looked something like pampas grass. I wondered out loud how you could possibly trim a tree like that. Someone said, 'Ask the Barnets, they have one of those trees.'"

Interpretation: "I think it's related to the houseguests again. Our old and dear friends—the Barnets—were coming to Santa Monica, and I was wishing I could get them persimmons from the tree at their former house here. But in addition to the fact that someone else owns the house, I couldn't even steal them because the branches were *too high.*"

Dream: "I was standing at a large reception for people associated with the County Community Colleges and suddenly saw Albert White. I made my way over to him in the crowd. I was anxious to find out how his new job was going, but I kept losing him in the crush of people (I am short)."

Interpretation: "(Still associations with the Modern Language anniversary.) We had a dinner party at our house for some of the visitors and my husband had lost track of one of the guests—and failed to bring him home to dinner. Everyone else at the dinner party had recalled seeing him at the large reception, but my husband had never run into him. He has changed jobs recently."

Dream: "I was traveling with a carnival. The caravan was made up of a series of hand-carved wooden coaches—all carefully tooled with elaborate designs—and all the coaches (in which we lived) were painted red. My role in the carnival was unclear—the focus of the dream was on the careful and elaborate hand-carving on each of the coaches."

Interpretation: "I think this may be hooked up to the fact that my friend Cindy is coming to visit. Cindy carved and sold beautiful chests to make a living after her husband was killed in the final days of the Korean War."

Freer access to one's dreams comes slowly, but it will happen with practice. The Inner Enemy is there—you will recognize it when it turns up. The most important thing is to add any new information to your dossier on the Inner Enemy. With luck, your dreams may even show you how to cope with the twerp—in fact, you may cope very well in your dreams. Your dreams are yet another way to mobilize information to fight the twerp, to look for clues that will heal the twerp-induced wounds. And they are a way to have fun and while away your time while drinking your morning coffee.

11

Twerp Control: Bringing the Heel to Heel

BECOMING AWARE OF the Inner Enemy and how it operates, raising one's consciousness with regard to it, is only half the battle of being more in control of one's inner life. Learning the skills and tactics to confront and fight the twerp is the second half of the twerp-management puzzle.

The exercises and techniques covered in this and the following chapter are neither difficult nor time-consuming. Many are just pointers or reminders of ways to contend with the twerp. Quite a variety of tactics are covered. This chapter concentrates on twerp-management skills, especially on rules, instructions, and tactics for holding fair debates and dialogues with the inner voices. Chapter 12 is about anti-twerp artillery—tactics, rituals, and tips for dealing with the Inner Enemy.

From your own experience and from the information and evidence you have gathered thus far, you should have a good idea of the strengths and weaknesses of your inner voices and your ability to manage them. By skimming through Chapters 11 and 12, you can determine what exercises to choose in devising a personal Twerp Control Plan. Your objective is a plan of action that will enable you to fight back when the Inner Enemy surfaces. By developing such a plan, you are taking a stand against the Inner Enemy and for yourself, your growth and satisfaction.

The Twerp Control Plan should suit your needs. Not only should you choose exercises that address your particular problems, but the plan should take into account the amount of time and effort you are willing to expend on combating the Inner Enemy. Don't tackle massive reforms you are bound to fall short of, or exercises that are uncomfortable for you. The battle with the Inner Enemy is fought in slow steps—it's infantry battle, not an air war. As you practice the exercises, you will be toughening up slowly but surely, building your immunity to twerp attacks. With practice, with reinforcement of these simple techniques, self-confidence grows and along with it the ability to take risks, to believe in the present reality and not the dim, defeating past. No longer need we feel helpless and unlovable under our smiling facades. The idea is to be tough with ourselves, tenderly. When the Inner Enemy is not so fearsome, we come to take a more tolerant and playful interest in ourselves. Our self-interest becomes more benign and flexible as opposed to rigid and self-critical. We do less of the kind of inverted, wallowing navel-gazing that keeps us from being able to attend to the other important people in our lives. Every bit we chip away from the Inner Enemy's stronghold allows us to turn outward a little more.

THE INGREDIENTS OF FAIR FIGHTING

In practice, each individual acts as the administrative executive of the voices that populate the Inner Parliament. If this responsibility is handled ineptly or neglected, the voices become unruly and incoherent, and those voices which ally themselves with growth and creativity are drowned out by the twerp's forces. An efficient executive is able to inspire teamwork among the individual voices, maintain order and discipline, assure and encourage fair debate. As monitor of the inner voices, the executive asserts control not through the use of strict rules and punitive measures, but by loosening up on the reins, letting all the voices be heard, being tolerant and accepting of the Inner Enemy's right to exist. Once you can free-associate with the twerp, you can freely associate with the twerp, without fear. If this is done in a safe, nonthreatening atmosphere where no below-the-belt punches are tolerated, the twerp has no chance to steal your thunder or reduce you to a quivering blob of protoplasm.

Keep in mind that you are trying to establish an atmosphere of goodwill in which to debate the twerp. You want it to adopt your tactics, so don't use its outrageous below-the-belt techniques. By behaving fairly toward the twerp—letting it have its say, listening to it, not twisting its words, sticking to the truth, you make it fight with your weapons. However, you must always be alert when dealing with the twerp. It can be terribly charming, terribly reasonable. You must be able to see beyond its smooth facade, actively look for and refute the flaws in its arguments, be on guard not to let insults and untrue statements slide by. And you must be braced for its innate hostility toward you and your dreams. If you can create a controlled and even-handed environment, it is easier to tolerate the paradoxes and complexity of the many voices. So your first task in taking control of the Inner Enemy is to be aware of your responsibility for seeing that things run smoothly.

SCHEDULING

Taking responsibility for which voices get to speak, and when and for how long, is a major part of your executive function. It is you who must be sure that everyone gets to have their fair say, that no one is summarily shouted down, that messages are clearly given and received, that supportive voices are called in for debate when the twerp gets obnoxious. When matters get one-sided, it is you who must call that Inner Parliament into session and maintain order. When the Inner Enemy is around, it will try to capture all the attention. It is up to you to abort the filibusters and round robins that threaten the democratic process. This can be done by ordering the long-winded voice to stop, by negotiating with it to give equal time to an opposing voice, or by agreeing to hear out the filibusterer at another time. Round robins—the broken records we have been hearing for years—especially should be stopped at the earliest opportunity.

Address the twerp directly: "You're taking too much time." "You're not the only one who has something to say." "Not while I'm in the middle of working. I'll talk to you later."

"I've learned that I can postpone the Inner Enemy's ravings till a more convenient and less damaging time. I was in Philadelphia a month ago to give a lecture and receive an award from my colleagues. As the hour of the lecture drew near, the twerp really started in on me. 'You have nothing important to say. They think you're a big blowhard. What has your contribution been? It's your friend who arranged the award, you've got them all fooled.' The creep wouldn't shut up. It got worse and worse as people came by to shake hands, to talk, and it was at a fever pitch as I started to speak. Finally I said, 'Shut up, dammit! Leave me alone while I do this. We'll talk later.' Miraculously, it went away. The speech went smoothly and I was able to accept the praise of my colleagues graciously. But, oh boy, on the train ride to New York, it started up again. Yet it wasn't so bad now that I had the success of the speech behind me, and it wasn't any longer in a position to mess up my performance."

EQUALIZE THE ADVERSARIES

The techniques of fair debate are quite simple. First, the adversaries must be evenly matched. When the Inner Enemy gets rambunctious, it's hard to stand up to it: "You fool, what makes you think you can get this report done by tomorrow morning? You've been putting it off forever, you haven't done a thing. Aren't you getting a headache? You have ten calls to make, and you have to pick up the kids, and you don't have a clear idea in your head about what you want to say. And you haven't done your research properly . . ." And so on. A meek little voice piping up occasionally to say, "Well, I did it last time, and every other time," or "I am *not* getting a headache," is not a worthy opponent.

When the twerp takes off on one of its tirades, stronger ammunition is called for. Don't be put off by the twerp's courtroom demeanor. It loves to show up just when you are under pressure and feeling most vulnerable, with lots of blame and guilt to unload. The thing to do is stop for a moment—call time out—while you muster your allies to talk back. Mentally go through your roster of ally voices to see who can be helpful here, who will provide opposing testimony and support. Prepare your response to the twerp: "What do you mean? I've never missed getting a report in on time. And I have a reputation for writing the best reports in the company. I hear what you're saying (a little placating doesn't hurt), but even though I don't have it down on paper, I know what I'm going to write. And my research has been thorough as usual. This may be the best report I've ever written."

Make it a habit to remember and store positive actions and commentary for debates with the twerp, especially about recurring issues. Then when it tries to catch you by surprise and tyrannize you, you will have a cache of positive information to fight back with.

Feedback: Fight the Inner Enemy Blow for Blow

Encourage conflict in a slow, rational manner. It is important to answer back before the twerp has a chance to build up a big head of steam. This lessens the threat of the twerp getting carried away so that you feel too weak and demoralized to put up a good fight.

Take turns speaking. Don't let the twerp ramble on. Match it comment for comment:

> TWERP: You're never going to win this tennis game.
>
> ALLY: I'm winning, aren't I?
>
> T: It'll never last.
>
> A: This is the last set, I'm way ahead.
>
> T: You always do this. You start out fine, then you lose your concentration.
>
> A: Not today. I'm right on top of it. And I beat him last week, too, remember?
>
> T: Are you kidding? Your serve will go any minute. Look—there, you blew it! That's the first of . . .
>
> A: Forget it. That's the only double fault you'll see. It's important for me to win this. To show you. Look! Practically an ace.
>
> T: But that's just the beginning. You look much more tired than he.
>
> A: You can't get me on the serve; now you tell me I'm tired. You're pathetic. I could go two more sets without breathing hard.

Constant monitoring and feedback in these situations works wonders. If the twerp had made all those comments without opposition, the tennis player would have been overwhelmed. But by standing up to this creepy street brawler and making it play fair, she was able greatly to soften the Inner Enemy's impact at this crucial time.

CLOSURE

Debates with the twerp should not be allowed to trail off into nothingness—out of exhaustion or because there is nothing more to say. An official recognition of the end of a dialogue or resolution is part of fair play. It might only be a matter of saying, "OK, that's enough for now," or "Let's talk tomorrow," or "You made a good point."

USING THE INNER DIALOGUE TO SELF-CONSULT AND SOLVE PROBLEMS

As the twerp comes more under control, it is possible to turn your attention to more constructive use of the Inner Dialogue. Rather than let the dialogue ramble at will, especially in nonproductive ways, it is possible to arrange specific debates, discuss current problems, or encourage debate between specific voices.

KEEPING A CLEAN RECORD

It is a good practice to clear the air as often as possible of any troubling situations in your present life before they have a chance to become entrenched, before they get blown out of proportion. Left unattended, they may become fodder for new twerp set pieces; they become fixtures in your Twerp Museum.

Select a current instance in which you felt you were stupid or hurtful or immoral, in which you felt something went wrong. It could be a very minor incident or a major goof-up: The idea is to prevent an accumulation of negative feelings, to keep barnacles from building up so that you can move forward smoothly. Pose the question:

> Why didn't I call Margaret?
> Why did I eat so much at lunch?
> Why did I yell at my son so harshly for such a small infringement of the rules?
> Why do I keep telling myself that my friend Maureen never has enough time for me?

Talk to yourself about what happened, try to get straightforward information. Don't let the enemy—the Spoiler or the Overindulger—run away with it. Be sure that your allies are around to make the fight fair.

For example:

> ALLY VOICE: Why didn't you call Margaret?
>
> ENEMY VOICE: I didn't feel like it.
>
> AV: No, that's not true. There was more to it than that.
>
> EV: Actually I was a little bored with her last time I saw her.
>
> AV: Oh, I thought you were pretty interested in her.
>
> EV: Well, yes. But I was so busy today. I didn't have a minute.
>
> AV: You could have found a minute. You're probably scared to call her.

EV: Why should I be? I'm never afraid to call women.

AV: Maybe you really like her.

EV: So. Why didn't I call her then?

AV: I'm telling you. You're shy. You're afraid of rejection.

EV: No. I'm pretty sure she liked me.

AV: Pretty sure.

EV: I'm sure. But I just didn't know exactly what to say.

AV: Ah ha. Now we're getting somewhere. Why don't you think about what you'll say.

EV: I didn't like to plan something like that. I like to be spontaneous.

AV: Well, keep on being spontaneous like this and you'll never talk to her again.

EV: I get the point. I'll think about it.

AV: OK. It's no crime to be shy. It just shows you're human after all.

EV: I'll call her tomorrow.

Once there is a clear understanding of the incident, let that be the end of it. This brief debate kept the issue from escalating and from being misinterpreted. Additionally, it gave this man insight into himself and presented a solution to a problem (his shyness) that he hadn't even recognized.

Putting an End to Long-Running Twerp Tapes

It is particularly important to clear the air when you have been punishing yourself with some long-running round-robin argument. If you're brooding over something you feel you did wrong, you must get yourself off the hook so that the twerp won't continue to store it in the arsenal for future self-esteem-destroying battles.

There are two steps to this process: One, accept the blame for whatever you feel you did wrong and reject all other accusations and insults the twerp throws at you. And two, articulate it: "It really was thoughtless of me to forget Karen's birthday. But I did send a late card. Besides, I was very busy this week, and otherwise I've been a good friend to Karen." This blame taking can be done in the course of a debate with the twerp; it puts the issue in perspective and keeps the twerp from piling too much recrimination or unwarranted criticism on you. This tactic is especially helpful for issues that have become clouded by years of persecution. Have it out with the Inner Enemy until you can cut through all the dramatics and exaggeration and see where the truth lies. It can be a great relief. Here's Arthur's story:

"For years—and I mean fifty years now—I have been haunted by a memory of taking my little sister to the circus—I was ten and she was seven—and scaring her by making her go too close to the elephants and then taunting her when she wet her pants. This is a vivid memory, mind you—I recall every detail of that circus and what took place—what we ate, what we wore, what I said to Cynthia. The memory of my behavior seemed so awful to me that I've always felt uncomfortable around my sister—even though we're close and there are no problems between us now. The twerp taunted me so much about this incident. It would depress me each time it came up; and the twerp was full of accusation. Finally I realized it was way out of proportion, and had it out with the twerp. I argued out loud, telling all the good things I had done with Cynthia, even that day we went to the circus. I was able to avoid for a change the twerp's total vindictiveness. Now I have a standard comeback whenever it begins to berate me about Cynthia. And already its attacks are losing their old vehemence."

The second part of the procedure for clearing the slate of blame and recrimination is to get yourself off the hook—to do penance or punish yourself—for what you realistically believe was wrong. This may sound foolish or harsh, but be assured that the twerp loves the jobs of judge and executioner. It will continue to punish you in its inimitable way, far longer and far out of proportion to your so-called crime.

When choosing your own penance, the punishment should *not* fit the crime. For two reasons: The crime is already blown out of proportion by the twerp; and *you* should be the one to determine the punishment, not it. Also, the deed for which you are doing penance may be long past.

In Arthur's case he did not atone for his treatment of his sister Cynthia by going out of his way to apologize or do things for her—he sentenced himself to spending a day cleaning and painting the basement of his house.

Punishment is a weapon used especially harshly by the twerp. By wresting this power from the Inner Enemy and by doling out rewards and punishment ourselves, we weaken its powers.

It is useful to have a set punishment ritual—as well as a reward ritual—to use when needed. It beats the twerp to the punch. Then when something goes wrong and you feel bad or guilty, you can use the ritual you have devised—rather than the twerp meting out the sentence, taunting you, causing you to drink too much or become depressed, whatever it does now to punish you. (See Reward and Punishment Rituals, pages 189–191.)

This technique should also be used for the reverse situation. It is all too easy to overlook or minimize the good things we do. Good deeds or accomplishments need equal time if we are to keep the twerp's voice in balance. Pick out current instances in which you did well, in which you were helpful or ethical or comforting. Again, pose the situation as a question and debate it:

> Why did I spend so much time helping Bea with her project outline?
> How did I win such a difficult tennis game?
> How was I able to resist all that fattening food at dinner?

In this case, of course, you should pat yourself on the back and reward your accomplishment, where appropriate. This is just one more way to encourage and reinforce the positive voices. (See Reward and Punishment Rituals, pages 189–191.)

A noteworthy addendum to Arthur's story: When Arthur decided to do something about the lasting guilt he felt about his sister, he checked out with Cynthia her memory of this incident. He did this almost as an afterthought, to clear the air between them and to be rid of this troublesome moment from his past.

Imagine his surprise to find her memory of the incident was very different, one in which he was nowhere near as malicious and mean as he remembered. Cynthia remembered that he had been wonderful to her all day at the circus, then mortified and ashamed when he realized how badly he had scared her. He had taken her to the rest room, helped her out of her wet pants, helped her wash, hugged her, apologizing profusely, and had gone out of his way not to tell their strict governess so she wouldn't get into trouble.

There is a lesson here. The Inner Enemy often rewrites history to fit its critical negative scenarios, to pick out only the bad things and blow them up out of proportion. It pays to be vigilant about this sort of distorted reporting of the past. When possible, check out those haunting memories—and confusing contemporary occurrences—as soon as possible with a fair witness, so as not to be misled.

ISSUES AND ANSWERS

The Inner Dialogue is also useful to use to debate ongoing issues, to gain insight into your thoughts and feelings about things that are important to you. Have a debate about:

The Way I Look.
Does _____ Love Me?
Will I Get Ahead in My Profession?
Am I an Honest Person?
What Is the Meaning of Life?
What Are My Goals?
What Should I Teach My Children?

You can also set up dialogues in which you match up opposing inner voices so that they learn to confront each other directly: the Procrastinator and the Go-getter, the Pessimist and the Optimist, the Scaredy-cat and the Adventurer, the Creator and the Stick-in-the-Mud.

In Tanya's dialogue with the Recluse and the Party Girl, she hears both voices out, she is able to negotiate with them for change and fair play. The dialogue helps her to understand her inner conflicts and to establish goodwill with her inner voices.

TANYA: Who's that droning on and on? Who are you? What do you want?

RECLUSE: I'm Recluse. I'm the loner part of you.

T: What do you want from me, Recluse?

R: The promise that you won't betray me again the way you did in your marriage, being so wishy-washy about stating when you needed time alone, going to dumb parties that you hated. I want that promise from you if I have to choke you to death to get it.

T: OK, Recluse, you got it. Now what do I want from you? I want you to make me a deeper person, a more daring and searching artist. I want you to give me strength and discipline to work long hours, to get done what I want to do and say what I want to say before I die. I want you to help me face my existential self with courage and not get derailed into dumb bullshit that throws me off-center. That's what I want from you, Recluse, Loner. Nothing less.

R: OK, Tanya, I'll try, but you have to stick with me. I can't work miracles overnight. You gotta hang in.

PARTY GIRL: Hey, what about *me*!!!????

T: What do you want?

PG: I want fun, goddamit, and girlish joy. Glamour and pretty clothes, popularity, people who want me, want me, want me, invite me to Paris for weekends or a London country home to make love, and ride into Stratford to see Shakespeare and picnic and screw some more, and rent me a room at the elegant Connaught Hotel and buy me beautiful lingerie. I want to get up on a table at a swell party and dance naked, sing and make everybody laugh. I want to be famous and rich and adorable. But you won't play, nasty Tanya. You never let me out to play, just two or three hours now and then, just a weekend at Wilbur Hot Springs or a week with a live-in lover in North Hollywood. You're a party pooper. I hate you.

T: I hate you, too. But wait a minute, Party Girl, what do I want from you? I don't know. I don't like you. I hate you.

PG: Ditto. Old Stick-in-the-Mud Tanya. Old boring Tanya. You're a drag. Full of rules and diets and exercises and goddam phony discipline that doesn't add up to two bits.

T: Well, Party Girl, I hate your materialism, your greed, your childishness and hedonistic obsessions, your conceit, your stupid goals like getting up on a table and dancing naked. How superficial! You're a Ginger Rogers movie. You're Betty Boop and I want no part of you. Get out!

PG: You know damn well you can't kick me out. I won't go. I'll cry on your doorstep all wrapped in wet confetti. I'll throw champagne corks at your windowpane. I'll stuff your garbage can with worn-out dancing shoes and used diaphragms.

T (*weeping*): Oh, Party Girl, help me. I'm so unhappy today. I cried all through my meditation session. Could you perhaps be my long-lost sister, Star? Related to Sarah Bernhardt and Eleanora Duse? My mother used to watch you when she was a little girl, sitting in the dark at the Opera House or the Odeon Theater. You played Camille with a wooden leg. You played Romeo and Hamlet and Rebecca of Sunnybrook Farm and Ben-Hur. You were alive, flesh and blood, and my mother used to be driven up from the farm into Chicago, an hour and a half on a dirt road when she was a little girl, to see you perform. Could you be Star, my long-lost sister?

PG: Yes, that's a part of me. My last name is Star.

T: Oh, Sister Star, help me. I'm so unhappy today. I don't want to get old, but I'm getting old. I don't want to be alone, but I'm alone.

PG (Star): You're not alone. You have your son.

T: Only for another three years.

PG: You have your therapist.

T: But I pay her.

PG: You have Barbara.

T: Barbara's married to Jim, and he comes first.

PG: You have Emil Dann.

T: Emil is married, too, and has Natalie. I'm close but not first.

PG: First, first, first! You're as greedy as me. You have your whole big pioneer Montana historical family.

T: Yes. They help in emergencies but we can't relate day-to-day.

PG: Why do you keep pining for community, Tanya, this *person*-lover as compared with object-lover? This really heavy Significant Other? Bullshit. That's no fun. That's a lot of work. Just screw-screw, Tanya. Don't think-think. Why aren't you satisfied with screw-screw?

T: Because everyone else has a partner and I feel abnormal without one. I feel amputated. Unsupported, outcast, weird. My son's schoolfriends tell him he has a weird mother. I feel old and scared. I don't want to die alone. I don't want never to make love again, but I don't want to just screw anymore. I want to be made love to. And I want to finish my book. And write some more. I want to write right now. Please leave me alone for a while, Party Girl. We'll continue this later.

BROKEN RECORDS, ROUND ROBINS, HABITS

The hardest twerp patterns to break are its one-sided, oft-repeated harangues. The inner soap opera, the round-robin arguments, the self-punitive habits are its specialties. The twerp's predictable but nonetheless devastating spiels about certain issues in your life are often repeated for years on end. It may be a diatribe about your weight, about how you treated your ex-boyfriend, about the job you messed up, about some small incident in the past. Or the Inner Enemy dwells on, wallows in, some current misfortune or unhappiness—loneliness or lack of money or unhappy marriage—so loudly and constantly that all constructive or supportive comment is smothered. These are the toughest twerp patterns to break because they have become so entrenched and we are weakened by them.

It is almost impossible to describe the power the Inner Enemy wields when it latches on to an issue, a weakness, or a fear. The turmoil and torment and disorientation it can cause are considerable. The time and energy wasted are enormous. And once started, it's very hard to stop it.

Here are some excerpts condensed from the journal Evelyn kept while taking the Inner Enemy course. Months after her separation from her husband, she is still overwhelmed by feelings of loneliness. Though Evelyn seems to want to put an end to her mourning and loneliness, the Inner Enemy has gotten into such a strong position and has established such a powerful hold that it's an uphill battle.

Sunday:
  7:00–7:15 Awoke and began to ruminate in bed—wonder what he is doing now—here I am again, unable to stay and sleep home on a Saturday

night, and so again at my friend's home—
will I ever begin to be able to sleep at home
on weekends—and he is not alone—

7:15–7:30   Stop! I got up and finished the rumination in
the bathroom—I have to go home today and
Sunday is always the worst—will I get those
lonely feelings when I get home as I usually
do when I am finally alone?—I have so
much work to do—I have to do the work
and not think—I will do my work for two
hours at night and then take a walk on the
beach—Stop!

12:30–12:40   As soon as I come home the aloneness is
creeping over me like a wave—all the memories—all ended—Stop! I begin to do my
laundry and water my plants.

4:00–4:15   After the timed work came the promised
walk on the beach—you have to go to your
chair for this—here I am all alone on a Sunday afternoon—poor me, why me?—it is
such a beautiful day and I am alone—democratic voice says—enjoy the peace and quiet
and beauty and continue to do your work—
you are OK and a good person. Autocratic
voice says—don't I feel lonely? And democratic voice says—I don't want to let myself
feel lonely—I don't need to feel lonely—
Stop! I continue my work for school, grad-
ing papers, planning.

9:30–10:00   Feel alone, school starting tomorrow, weekend ending and he didn't call. I know it's
over—turned on TV—turned off TV.

10:00–10:15   Anger: WHY did I begin to think about him
as soon as I awoke?—why can't I get up one
morning without him on my mind?—I get so
angry with you when you pity yourself—but

proud that you got a good amount of work done and you did enjoy the time by yourself today—you had to call only one friend—and you had dinner at home. I feel good.

Monday:

5:15–5:30   Awoke after dreaming of my husband and my sister [she is in South America], and felt very alone, missing them both—rumination begins—it's so hard to get up—my reality is that I am alone—why can't I get used to it?—when will the pit in my stomach go away?—always when I get up I don't have much time because I have to get up for work—wish I could go back to sleep for these next five minutes—I'll try—I can't—Stop! I began to get ready for work.

8:45–8:50   During my teaching break—I am lonely—why does everyone have someone and not me?—why does everyone appear to be so happy except me? Stop! My democratic voice says—maybe they are and you will be, too—you have work to do and you do it well.

2:20–2:30   After my classes were over—my laissez-faire self, feeling apathetic, tired and alone but don't care.

9:30–10:00   Anger: You did it again, Evelyn, as soon as you got up, you allowed dreams to affect you and again felt lonely, despairing, but you did get over it sooner—only ten minutes this time and it's OK to feel like that, especially after dreams of the ones who you love and are not here with you. I wrote my sister today.

Tuesday:

5:15–5:30   Awoke with pit of loneliness in my stomach after dreams again—he didn't call last night as he usually does—it is over—why?—we had so much and now it's over. I feel my chaotic side taking over—all confused, thinking of so many things at once—why doesn't he get psychological help?—I am the one getting help and he is the one that is a mess—God, I think it will be all over soon and I don't know how to stop it—but do I want to stop it?—I didn't do any work last night—I'd better get up and get to school early—chaos is taking over—Stop! I got up and started preparing for school.

2:15–2:30   Aloneness after my classes are over—had time to think of him and that we would never be together again—will I ever meet anyone else? My democratic voice says, yes, someday, but don't think of that now—Stop! I begin to grade papers and then walk around, visiting friends in their classrooms.

10:00   Anger: I began same self-pity tape this morning, but I did cut it down from ten to five minutes.

Wednesday:

5:20–5:25   Awoke with pit in stomach—feeling of aloneness. He didn't call—I can't call him—he must be ready to call me—I miss him—he probably thinks of me but doesn't miss me—I wish I could meet someone else—I will, I hope—I have to have patience—sometimes I feel all alone—Stop! I got up and began to get ready for school.

2:00–2:05   After my classes are over and I start to relax, I begin to feel alone—he still hasn't called. I miss him and he doesn't seem to miss me at all—I wish I could find someone else—Stop! I'm OK—I'm healthy, and I'll be all right. I went to talk with other teachers in lounge.

9:00–9:10   As I was eating ice cream by myself, watching TV, I felt alone—no calls and ruminations began—went to my special chair—it's over—Stop! Anger: I still feel sorry for myself—I got up this morning and started to feel sorry for myself—I wish I would stop and think how lucky I am to be healthy and have a profession I enjoy, and a place to live, but I am proud of myself for seeing the positive side sooner—the side that said I'm OK and I'll be OK—the aloneness did go away sooner.

Thursday:

5:15–5:20   I awoke with pit in my stomach—decided to get up right away and write my thoughts down before my tape begins—I still feel the pit as I'm writing this, but I'm starting to get ready for school—no time to ruminate now!

It is easy to become practically hypnotized by the Inner Enemy's repeated assaults, especially when they have gone on for a long time. We may become so disheartened at our seeming inability to fight back that we give up the moment we hear the old familiar refrain start up. We can't even muster the strength to tell it to shut up.

How do you break this vicious circle? By using every means in the anti-twerp arsenal (Chapter 12). And by fighting fire with fire. The Inner Enemy's diatribe is consuming a disproportionate amount of time and energy. You must try to reclaim some of the territory occupied by the issue in question, and the best way is by developing an equally powerful "act." Calling on the ally voices, looking at the twerp-free areas of your life, you must gather material that refutes the Inner Enemy's point of view, amass a body of evidence that supports your best interests. Write everything down so you have the information handy the next time the broken record starts to play again. Develop your own spiel—logical, showy, convincing—so you are worthy competition for the twerp.

"I'm proud of the way I handled my divorce. I wasn't intimidated by Ned's threats. I set myself up with job interviews within a month. I was fair, even though I was angry, about visiting rights with the kids, and I don't say anything bad about him to them. I'm learning to spend time alone, and I'm starting to meet men again and will probably be dating soon. There are friends I can call and spend time with. I can laugh at my mistakes. I've come a long way in just a few months."

Rehearse it. Embellish it. Then every time the issue comes up—whether every day, every hour, or just every time you take time off for yourself—give the twerp back its own medicine. As we use the new spiel over and over, as it becomes more repetitious and set, it, too, becomes a broken record but a positive one, a powerful weapon in offsetting the relentless nagging of the Inner Enemy.

Bad habits are definite signs of the twerp at work. Drinking, smoking, compulsive lateness, spending too much money, these are some of the twerp's favorites—they are really harmful. And they should be attacked in the same way—by developing a specific counterattack.

"I've been working at curbing my spending habits, which were getting more and more destructive. It was getting to the point where my answer to the slightest problem was to buy something—anything—although I'd always have a reason for it. I got a headache from reading, so I should have a new reading lamp. It would be easier if I had a second camera and lenses to keep at the office. Good brandy is a luxury worth having—there was a reason for everything. Then I realized that whenever anything went wrong—and even when things didn't go wrong—a little voice in my head would say, 'What you need is _____.' It was like a slogan, it never varied.

"Now I've learned to retort immediately, 'I have everything I need.' I say exactly that, every time. And as the debate continues I make sure I have something to say at every opportunity. I list the things I have. I ridicule what the twerp says I need, 'What would I do with another tape recorder?' I've also changed other things. I used to keep a lot of cash on hand—another clever twerp trick—so that it was easy for me to spend on impulse. Now I keep the bare minimum, and I have only one charge account. This is still a battle for me, but every time I resist, it makes it easier the next time. And it gives me new ammunition to confront the twerp with."

12

Twerp Control: Anti-Twerp Artillery

THE INNER ENEMY has a vast store of ammunition it can use on you. It remembers everything you have done wrong, every embarrassing moment, every fumble and moment of panic. It saves juicy tidbits of gossip, shattered dreams, chances not taken. Weakness, flaws, pimples, Achilles' heels, unsavory behavior are all carefully catalogued. And the twerp can muster this information at any time. Sometimes the barrage is so unexpected, so heavy, so relentless that we are stunned—shell-shocked and powerless to counterattack. The best defense is to amass your own arsenal to fight the twerp, to be prepared when it comes to battle. There are several kinds of anti-twerp weaponry. Many are for use in the course of the Inner Dialogue, to augment debates and encourage fair fighting. Others, incorporated into your everyday life, help strengthen allies, build self-esteem, and draw energy and attention away from the twerp and toward more positive thought and action.

ANTI-TWERP FILES

Not only does the twerp have extensive dossiers on all the bad things about you, but the information is packaged and stored so that it can be called up at will and presented in a way carefully calculated to wound. The way to counter this kind of attack is to assemble your own files concerning the issues the twerp tends to hound you about. For every one of these vulnerable spots, you must accumulate data that refute the twerp's arguments. Make a list of all the areas in which you are competent. All the reasons why you are good at your job, why you are not intimidated by meeting new people. All the good things you do for your kids, all the ways in which your spouse shows that he or she cares. Collect evidence to support your thesis. Add information to the files as you think of it or discover it. Review these files from time to time, so that when you need the information, and when the twerp has you on the spot, you don't have to grope for a comeback.

As you do battle with the twerp, as you tune in more and more to the Inner Dialogue, you will find that the twerp has vulnerabilities, too. It will back down on certain issues, shut up at certain times, be intimidated by particular remarks. Note these items in the files. As time goes by, the Inner Enemy's territory will slowly shrink, and you should be alert and ready to move allies into vacated areas in order to actively reinforce good feelings and actions as these areas open up to healthy growth.

Rehearsals

The twerp has a tendency to turn up when we are having a good time or in the midst of something important, and make a shambles of it. Anticipation of this kind of activity is your best defense. By now you are likely aware of many of the situations in which the twerp is wont to cause trouble. You can soften its impact in many instances by being prepared; specifically by going over the situation in your mind and thinking through what is likely to happen, by thinking about what you can do to counter the twerp's interference.

It may be a simple matter of reminding yourself that when you are introduced to your new coworkers tomorrow, you will be nervous and likely to forget their names, so you should pay special attention.

Maybe you have to remind yourself that when you take pictures of your daughter's graduation next week, you should not forget to change the setting on your camera as you have done before on important occasions.

Rehearsing a difficult situation can be helpful. Plan exactly what you are going to say when you tell your daughter she can't go on the overnight trip with her friends. Think through similar past situations so you can anticipate what will be difficult for you, what questions and arguments will come up, and where the twerp will interfere. It is often helpful to simulate this kind of situation by having a friend play the role of your daughter.

If the twerp has a way of spoiling a good time for you, remind yourself that this is likely to happen—and exactly how—then think about what you can do specifically to avoid this when you go to that party (or other social event).

Be prepared for the feeling of dread that sets in whenever you sit down to write or paint or plan a new project. It is better than being caught unawares—over and over again—and being too anxious to work.

REWARD AND PUNISHMENT RITUALS

An effective way to steal the Inner Enemy's thunder is to take away its power to punish. The twerp has its own punishments specially tailored to each person. It makes one person depressed and anxious, it drives another to drink or drugs; it causes another person to worry constantly, unproductively, someone else to give up what he really wants for safety or security, or another person always to doubt and undermine others' love.

By developing a personalized punishment ritual that can be used whenever we feel guilty, whenever we feel we have done wrong, we short-circuit the Inner Enemy's power to punish us. We diminish its scope or influence and the unpredictability of the punishment. Also, the twerp is likely to discipline us severely and out of proportion to the "crime."

With a personal punishment ritual, you become your own judge and administrator. The ritual should be used whenever *you* feel it is needed, especially in connection with the kind of inner dialogue described in Chapter 11.

It doesn't particularly matter what the ritual is. It should be something unpleasant or onerous—but not something demeaning. And it should be something with a fixed time limit. Make a list of several things you hate to do—perhaps one will stand out—so that whenever punishment is in order, you will immediately be able to choose and administer it and not let the twerp beat you to the punch.

Sample punishment rituals:

> Wash the floors.
> Clean the closets.
> Write five overdue letters.
> Give up taxis for a week.
> Skip the weekly movie and do the laundry.
> Do all the mending.
> Update the tax records or pay the bills.
> Give up the weekly golf or poker game.

It also pays to have a reward ritual. One reason the twerp is so powerful is that most people tend to overlook the good things they do, while paying plenty of attention to the bad. Accomplishments or good deeds generally pass unheralded, so they count less when the balance is being toted up. If we are to ally with the positive forces within us, we must beef them up and mark the occasions when they pull ahead. Reward rituals should especially be used when we succeed in overcoming the twerp—no matter how small the victory. Again, making a list of rewards will help. Just be sure to use them.

Sample reward rituals:

A movie or the theater—keep a running list of shows to see so you can make an immediate choice.

A long bath.

A meal in a favorite restaurant.

An evening alone to read and relax.

A special purchase—keep a list of things you would like to have.

A half hour off to take a walk.

A long-distance call to a friend.

TWERP RETORTS

The twerp is a trickster, full of ploys, surprises, and gimmicks. We can borrow a trick from it by developing little ploys of our own that serve to temper, pacify, or refute the Inner Enemy's power.

One of the twerp's favorite tactics is a hook—a special example in the vulnerable areas of your life—that it harps on and uses as a screen to distract you from seeing the broader picture. The twerp has a special "downer" that relates to your looks, another that has to do with your career or competence, or one that concerns your health or your lovability. In any area the twerp will focus on that one wart, that *pièce de résistance,* until it seems to obliterate everything else. Simple but effective. And the most effective counterattack is to develop an "upper," a positive hook that you can focus on and harp on in the same boring way.

In each area where the Inner Enemy picks at you with a redundant downer, choose the most upbeat, concrete, solid counterargument you can think of and use it. If the twerp drives you to distraction about your mousy hair, remind it *every time* it does so about your high cheekbones or wide-set green eyes or graceful hands, or whatever. If the twerp focuses on the colds you get so often, remind it *every time* that you haven't spent a day in bed since you were in the fifth grade. If it chides you about getting your work done late, remind it *every time* that you are the youngest executive in the company, or that you have written four published articles, or anything else you can think of.

Be very specific about these twerp retorts. Refine the exact phraseology you are going to use and never vary it. The twerp is a fascist. It knows the propaganda value of sloganeering, the hypnotic effect of a repeated litany or chant:

> Late again. Always behind the eight ball.
> There I go again. Same stupid mistake.
> All she cares about is her clothes and her allowance.
> One more drink won't do any harm.

Your own retorts should be equally catchy and on the tip of your tongue, ready to be flung back at the twerp at a moment's notice:

> Three promotions in two years. Not bad.
> That portrait I did of Jane is sensational.
> I haven't forgotten my keys in ten years.
> My kids really love me.
> I've really stuck to this diet.

It helps as well to have a few general slogans to throw at the Inner Enemy when it gets out of hand:

> Every dog will have his day.
> I'll talk to you when I'm good and ready.
> You're cute when you're riled.

Whatever catchphrases you choose, use them as often as possible, in the same repetitive, bludgeoning manner that the twerp employs so effectively.

Joy Triggers

The Inner Dialogue of many people—their dreams, memories, and daydreams—is overrun with negative material. It dwells on misfortune, it wallows in misery, it is plagued by memories of things gone wrong, opportunities missed, disastrous mistakes. The balance of good and bad, positive and negative, is seriously out of whack. The prominent memories, the repeated tapes and round robins, are more likely to be scenarios of misery than of joy. Pleasant memories do not seem to get imprinted the way the bad ones do.

It is just another way the Inner Enemy has of keeping people in thrall. As long as they focus on the negative, they are too anxious, too lacking in self-esteem, too closed to the satisfactions they might seek, to make changes in their lives. They stagnate.

The antidote to the twerp's joylessness is to seek out actively those things that make us feel good, rekindle those memories that make us smile. Once we remember or discover what gives us joy, we can use these things in the same repetitious manner the twerp uses to bring up bad news. We can call upon these "joy triggers" when we need them, use them to reinforce good feelings about ourselves and our lives.

A joy trigger can take many forms. It might be a memory—of a family gathering, of your first kiss, of receiving good news, of winning a prize. It might be a smell—of bread baking, of oil paint or leather, of the lilacs that grew in the yard. It might be a piece of music, a painting, a gift from a friend, a shell, a piece of jewelry, the view from your window.

Whatever it is that gives you pleasure, whatever can provoke those good feelings, use them. Make them part of the anti-twerp arsenal. Make a list of all the things you can think of, even the most trivial. Pick out the ones that are most meaningful to you and incorporate them in your life. Keep the nostalgic picture on your desk, not buried in the closet. Make a point of looking at it several times during the day, especially when you're bogged down. If you remember loving Chopin's nocturnes, get a record of them and play it every day, especially when things are going badly. Fix in your mind that memory of your first date with your spouse or lover; think about it over and over, especially when the twerp shows up to bedevil you. Tap those unconscious wells of joy. Lingering joy beats lingering misery.

Some sample joy triggers:

"I keep a favorite picture of my girlfriend on my desk. When things get hectic, when the phones don't stop ringing, when I get stumped on a problem, it's like stumbling on an oasis to look at that picture."

"Not a day goes by that I don't relive in my mind the surprise birthday party my friends threw for me last year when I was feeling 'all alone.'"

"I use a painted ceramic ashtray that my son made in school when he was six to keep soap in next to the sink. It never fails to cheer me."

"When I'm unappreciated, down, or uninspired, I remember the day I learned that I'd won a case I worked on for five years, and thought, 'How sweet it is.'"

"I love the smell of tangerines. I buy small vials of tangerine oil at the health food store and use the oil as perfume, so it's always with me."

"Whenever I look through our photo album, I'm filled with good memories. It's worth the effort of keeping it up to date."

"The cup that I drink my tea from each morning never fails to make me feel good. It's beautiful, delicate, colorful; it's a pleasure to hold and behold."

DAILY CLOSURES

It is helpful to take a couple minutes at the end of the day to evaluate how the inner enemies and allies are doing. Is there a balance, or is the Inner Enemy getting out of hand? Use this time to itemize any gains made by friendly voices. List accomplishments, happy or constructive dreams and daydreams. Congratulate yourself. Reinforce those supportive voices. If the twerp has been obnoxious, call a halt: "Enough" or "Time out." Do this especially if you're planning to go out for a pleasant evening, or if you're looking forward to something special that the twerp would love to spoil.

STRENGTHENING ALLIES

Strengthening one's inner allies is the best insurance the twerp won't be able to run amok and wreak havoc in one's life. Also, having supportive, interesting inner friends makes for a richer inner life, makes us feel comfortable with ourselves. Everyone inevitably has periods when he is alone. A person with strong Inner Allies accepts this and is able to sustain and nurture himself through these times. A person with a powerful Inner Enemy sees this loneliness as a personal failure. Part of loneliness is not feeling at ease with ourselves, not having the resources to entertain and interest ourselves, or feeling alien and at war with ourselves. For if the Inner Dialogue is against us, if there is more criticism than praise, more stagnation than growth, we have nowhere to turn when things go wrong in the outside world.

The Inner Enemy gets a good deal of our attention; it's always ranting about something, always getting in our way.

Inner allies, on the other hand, are all too often taken for granted, overshadowed and outshouted by the twerp. When things go smoothly, we accept it unquestioningly; it's when things go wrong that we pay attention. Bad news drives out good news.

It's for this reason that we are less familiar, less intimate with our inner allies; we just haven't spent that much time with them. It's no wonder that the allies tend to get talked down in the Inner Dialogue. Their voices are weaker; and our ears are less attuned to them.

Our companionable voices need to be cultivated and supported. We can do this by consciously singling out these voices for attention as we tune in on the Inner Dialogue. With practice we can learn to tune out the twerp talk and turn up the volume on our vital supporters. They have as much to say as the Inner Enemy, but they have been neglected. In time, we learn who these voices are, how they encourage and support us, in what situations they show up. And despite whatever tendencies we have to doubt their praise, we must learn to give them credit, to act on their advice, even though it runs counter to the twerp. Although it may seem silly, we should praise and compliment and thank these supporters effusively whenever they come to our aid. Devise standard compliments: "That was terrific." "You're a great friend." "When you hit your stride, you sure turn out great work." This is, after all, no more foolish than the browbeating tirades we direct against ourselves when the twerp is on stage.

The idea is to enlarge the twerp-free arenas in our lives, to usurp the twerp's territory. When we know who our inner friends are and know we can count on them, they can be rallied to combat the Inner Enemy. When the Procrastinator shows up, we can call on the Go-getter and say, "*You* talk to him." We can use the Adventurer to argue against the Scaredy-cat, can use our Buddy to neutralize the effects of the Saboteur.

SHARING THE INNER DIALOGUE

It is all too easy to get mired in that soap opera that goes on in our heads all the time if we never share our thoughts and concerns with others. Often the inner babble seems so weird and chaotic—even frightening—that we are loath to share it with anyone else. Perhaps they would think us strange or unbalanced. Perhaps we feel we'll be exploited by others if they know our failings, or judged harshly for our weaknesses. The danger of keeping our own counsel in this case is that without the perspective of others, and the burden-sharing, the twerp can run wild, secure in the knowledge that we think we are the only people in the world with this peculiar madness.

Supportive friends are a powerful weapon against the Inner Enemy. One of the first benefits of sharing some of the Inner Dialogue with others is that we learn we are not alone. Everyone lives with the same confusing, complex babble of voices, though the voices may be different and their effects may vary. It's a relief to have a friend with whom we can trade twerp stories, with whom we can compare twerps. When we can tell tales on ourselves without being embarrassed or ashamed, when we're able to laugh with others about the twerp's machinations, the twerp itself becomes laughable and less intimidating.

Another benefit is that sharing the Inner Dialogue brings us closer to others. They seem more real to us and we to them. It's a great boost to our self-esteem to see that they care for us even with our warts; perhaps they care more, or more appropriately. It's a relief—for our friends as well as ourselves—when we can shed the image of total confidence and competence at times. And out from under the pressure to live up to unrealistic expectations, we are likely to perform better and be less at the mercy of the Inner Enemy's ranting about our being impostors.

We should be choosy about those with whom we share the Inner Dialogue—our dreams, our goof-ups, the nagging voices, the daydreams. They should be people who are supportive of us, who think well of us, and who encourage us in pursuing our goals. Who needs friends who are as destructive and traitorous as the Inner Enemy? This is where the Inner Enemy comes from in the first place. Yet many people have friends and family members who belittle their behavior, who trivialize their dreams, and who turn what they say against them. They hear twerp talk from inner *and* outer voices. No wonder they learn to keep to themselves. Some people are so inured to criticism that they tend to underestimate or disbelieve the positive opinions of those who care for them. They listen more closely to the "friend" who is critical than to the friend who praises. Part of conquering the Inner Enemy is to learn to listen and give credence to those who support your inner allies. In fact, it's a good idea to look at our friends and family to see if they share some of the encouraging, helpful good-natured qualities of our inner allies or whether they tend to mimic the twerp.

"My wife always has something good to say about me, and is full of congratulations and praise for whatever I do. Yet somehow I tend to undervalue it and think it doesn't mean much—that she's just 'that way.'

"My friend Cal on the other hand is always finding fault, picking apart what I say, running down my accomplishments. Yet I listen to him. I came to believe his opinion was valuable and accurate. It took me a long time to recognize that Cal is jealous and consequently out for revenge. In fact, his voice sounds like one of my own insulting inner voices—it says the same things. Who needs it? I've learned to shrug off Cal's remarks—in fact, I see less of him. And, of course, I realize that my wife's support is not only informed and to the point, it's *good* for me."

When people are used to keeping to themselves, it's hard to break through the barrier of privacy to a more intimate sharing of thoughts and concerns. But this can be done slowly, in small doses, with someone trustworthy. It's not as though we have to tell all—there are many things we are more comfortable keeping to ourselves. And there are different things to share with different people.

The Walk/Talk discussed in Chapter 10 is a good way to break through inhibitions about talking with others about personal things. The walk is a pleasant way to share time with a friend; even if nothing is said, people feel closer for the shared experience. It's not necessary to air a particular problem, or discuss anything relating to the friend in question. It's just a sharing of thoughts, of getting bottled-up feelings off your chest, or trying out an idea:

"I had such an unproductive day; it was frustrating. The phone rang far too much, and I kept tripping over myself. Forgetting things. Losing things. Getting tongue-tied when I tried to talk to Joanne. It got so bad that I finally just gave up on the day—declared a truce. It was obvious I wasn't going to accomplish anything. I had to laugh at myself. I didn't know why it happened. Maybe I'm more worried than I thought about having that tooth pulled tomorrow. Or about Sally going away to school. Anyway, I should have just gone out and played tennis instead of brooding about it. Instead I wasted the whole day."

Your friend may not have much feedback for you in the way of advice; that's not the point. But the sympathetic ear has great therapeutic value.

The Walk/Talk is a device to bring ease to this new situation, but as it becomes more comfortable, it is possible to share the Inner Dialogue more often, more spontaneously, with those around us.

MAKING A TWERP CONTROL PLAN

Action is the key to twerp control. It's not enough to learn about the twerp and how it operates. What is crucial is to *do* something about it. The Twerp Control Plan is nothing more than an articulation of what you are going to do to combat the twerp. Your Twerp Control Plan should be based on what you have learned so far about your own twerp, which areas and situations feel most threatening to you, or which you feel are most amenable to change. It should also reflect the time and effort you are willing to devote to coping with the twerp, and the kind of action you are comfortable with.

The plan should be personal—a reflection of your needs and temperament—and realistic. Don't attempt more than you can handle and set yourself up for failure. The plan might be a combination of things—one or two exercises you feel will be helpful, a decision to set aside a few minutes a day for daydreaming, a slogan that you commit to using a number of times each day. Review the questions asked and information gathered in Chapters 7 through 9 to help you formulate an appropriate, effective plan. Whatever the plan is, write down your intentions on the form at the end of this chapter.

The plan should be detailed and specific. Refer to it at least once a day to keep your goals firmly in mind. From time to time revise it to reflect changes in your twerp, in your allies, and in your current needs.

A sample Twerp Control Plan:

1. I will take a Walk/Talk three times each week—about twenty minutes from the office, through the park (then pick up the bus on Grand Street). After I get used to this, I'll invite _____ to come along and see if ˙ can talk with him about the Inner Enemy.

2. Set aside five minutes each day for daydreaming. If something's on my mind, I'll use that for the subject of my daydreaming.

3. Allow five minutes each day to write down what I remember of the Inner Dialogue in a notebook—a small one which I'll carry with me.

4. The most destructive thing I'm doing now is staying in my job, not doing anything about opening a fishing camp, a fishing supply or sporting-goods store, or any of the things I used to dream about. I need to find out more about what the inner voices are saying, more about what my fears are. I need to make more positive plans, make lists of reasons and resources for me to start a new business, of supportive friends: I need "anti-twerp" files in this area.

5. Every time I get down on myself about my job, I'm going to say, "I'm working on going fishing."

TWERP CONTROL PLAN

1. _____
_____
_____
_____
_____

2. _____
_____
_____
_____
_____

3. _____
_____
_____
_____
_____

4. _____
_____
_____
_____
_____

5. _____
_____
_____
_____
_____

I will revise and review this plan on _____.

(date)

Date: _____   Signature: _____

13

Aggression in Service of the Self

THE RESULT OF learning to cope with the Inner Enemy is not, as might be wished, a twerp-free inner life. Rather, it is an active, healthy Inner Dialogue in which not so much is hidden, there are fewer secrets, there is a balance of positive and negative voices, and the Inner Enemy's power to terrorize and tyrannize is greatly reduced.

The Inner Dialogue is the clearinghouse for our thoughts, ideas, concerns, and feelings. By learning to process them efficiently and fairly, we reap tremendous rewards:

(1) *We are at ease with ourselves.* We accept the complexities, the contradictions, the paradoxes of our thoughts. The mixed meanings, the multiple messages become a source of interest rather than confusion. We take a benign, friendly, more tolerant interest in ourselves, and are therefore more available to others, able to transfer our defenses from those of power to love. We are able to amuse and entertain ourselves, to enjoy time spent alone, to comfort ourselves when necessary.

(2) *We learn about ourselves.* The Inner Dialogue has a

powerful educational function. The ability to have more and more access to the inner workings of our minds allows us to observe ourselves, to discover who we are, to differentiate ourselves from others, to sort out image and expectation from reality and desire. We learn to distinguish the truth about ourselves, to believe in what we see and hear, and are not misled and confused by the Inner Enemy's distortions of reality, by its denials of our own experience. We welcome revelations about ourselves. In coming to grips with who we are, we learn to accept our anger, to understand its source, and to relinquish the guilt we feel over this anger. Access to the Inner Dialogue demystifies the psychological explanations that seem too distant and depersonalized. Access to the Inner Dialogue reduces our anger at ourselves and increases our self-respect.

(3) *We use the Inner Dialogue constructively.* Once we know how to tune in to the Inner Dialogue, take more control of it, and are no longer afraid of it, we can actively call upon it. The dialogue becomes a tool for self-consultation. We can use it for advice and counsel, to think through specific situations, to plan—for dinner, or for the next ten years. We can call upon it to clarify our thoughts and actions, to spark creativity, to draw conclusions. An active Inner Dialogue seethes with ideas and opinions, dreams and hypotheses, which we can harness.

(4) *We are able to realize our dreams.* An active Inner Dialogue makes it possible to strip away some of the barnacles that slow us down as we try to move ahead; we are less likely to hit snags and obstacles. Better able to cope with our world, free of unproductive anxiety, we recognize the exorbitant price we have paid for conforming—for not being ourselves. No longer do we feel guilty about pursuing our own goals; we use our intelligence, our skills, and our aggression for, rather than against, ourselves. We have the wherewithal to become the person we dream of being.

Bibliography

Araoz, Daniel L. "Negative Self-Hypnosis." *Journal of Contemporary Psychotherapy*, 12:1 (Spring/Summer 1981), pp. 45–52.

Bach, George R. "The George Bach Self-Recognition Inventory for Burned-Out Therapists." *Voices: The Art and Science of Psychotherapy* (date unavailable), pp. 73–76.

———. "Spouse Killing: The Final Abuse." *Journal of Contemporary Psychotherapy*, November/December 1980.

———, and Yetta Bernhard. *Aggression Lab: The Fair Fight Training Manual.* Dubuque, Iowa: Kendal/Hunt Publishing Company, 1971.

———, and Ronald M. Deutsch. *Pairing.* New York: Avon Books, 1971.

———, and Deutsch. *Stop! You're Driving Me Crazy.* New York: G. P. Putnam's Sons, 1979.

———, and Herb Goldberg. *Creative Aggression.* New York: Avon Books, 1974.

———, and Laura Torbet. *A Time for Caring.* New York: Delacorte Press, 1982.

Bakan, David. "Belief and the Management of Chronic Pain." *Journal of Humanistic Psychology*, 20:4 (Fall 1980), pp. 37–44.

Benderly, Beryl Lieff. "Thinking: The Multilingual Mind," ("Thinking" feature). *Psychology Today* (March 1981), pp. 9–12.

Bettelheim, Bruno. "Reflections: Freud and the Soul." *The New Yorker* (March 1982), pp. 52–93.

Branden, Nathaniel. *The Psychology of Romantic Love.* Los Angeles: Tarcher, 1980.

——. *The Psychology of Self-Esteem.* Los Angeles: Nash Publishing Company, 1969.

Brandt, Anthony. "What It Means to Say No." *Psychology Today* (August 1981), pp. 70–77.

Bronfenbrenner, Urie. *The Ecology of Human Development.* Boston: Harvard University Press, 1979.

Brown, Norman O. *Life Against Death: The Psychoanalytical Meaning of History.* New York: Vintage Books, 1959.

Burka, Jane B., and Lenora M. Yuen. "Mind Games Procrastinators Play." *Psychology Today,* 16:1 (January 1982), pp. 32–37, 44.

Carnegie, Dale. *How to Stop Worrying and Start Living.* New York: Simon and Schuster, 1944.

Chetwynd, Tom. *How to Interpret Your Own Dreams (In One Minute or Less).* New York: Bell Publishing Company, 1980.

Cousins, Norman. *Anatomy of an Illness.* New York: W. W. Norton, 1979.

Davies, Nigel. *Human Sacrifice: In History and Today.* New York: William Morrow and Company, Inc., 1981.

Emery, Cedric, and George R. Bach. *Fight for Your Life: How to Get the Most Out of Your Doctor.* New York: Playboy Press, 1982.

Emmons, Michael L. *The Inner Source: A Guide to Meditative Therapy.* San Luis Obispo, California: Impact Publishers, 1978.

Gaylin, Willard. *Feelings: Our Vital Signs.* New York: Harper and Row, 1979.

Goldberg, Herb. *The New Male: From Self-Destruction to Self-Care.* New York: William Morrow and Company, Inc., 1979.

Greenwald, Harold. *Direct Decision Therapy.* San Diego, California: EdITS Publishers, 1973.

Greer, Frank L. "Toward a Developmental View of Adult Crisis: A Re-examination of Crisis Theory." *Journal of Humanistic Psychology,* 20:4 (Fall 1980), pp. 17–29.

Hilgard, Ernest. *Divided Consciousness.* New York: John R. Wiley, 1977.

Jaffe, Dennis T., and David E. Bresler. "The Use of Guided Imagery as an Adjunct to Medical Diagnosis and Treatment," *Journal of Humanistic Psychology,* 20:4 (Fall 1980), pp. 45–59.

Janeway, Elizabeth. *Powers of the Weak.* New York: Alfred A. Knopf, 1980.

Kleinke, Chris L. "Self-Labeling of Bodily States." *Journal Supplement Abstract Service Pamphlet.* Arlington, Virginia: American Psychological Association, 1977.

Kovel, Joel. *The Age of Desire: Case Histories of a Radical Psychoanalyst.* New York: Pantheon, 1981.

Kushner, Harold S. *When Bad Things Happen to Good People.* New York: Schocken Books, 1981.

Lasch, Christopher *The Culture of Narcissism: American Life in an Age of Diminishing Expectations.* New York: W. W. Norton, 1979.

Lazarus, Richard. "Little Hazards Can Be Hazardous to Health." *Psychology Today* (July 1981), pp. 58–62.

Lears, T. J. Jackson. *No Place of Grace: Antimodernism and the Transformation of American Culture 1880–1920.* New York: Pantheon, 1981.

Leo, John. "Therapy for Ethnics: Troubled Adults Seek Treatment with Their Own Kind." *Time* (March 15, 1982), p. 42.

Lindgren, Henry Clay. *How to Live with Yourself and Like*

It. Greenwich, Connecticut: Fawcett Publications, Inc., 1959.

McKenzie, Clancy D., and Lance S. Wright. "The Consciousness Movement, Silva Mind Control, and the Mental Patient." *Voices: The Art and Science of Psychotherapy,* 17:1 (Spring 1981), pp. 56–64.

McLuhan, Marshall, and Quentin Fiore. *The Medium Is the Massage—An Inventory of Effects.* New York: Bantam Books, 1967.

Malcolm, Janet. *Psychoanalysis: The Impossible Profession.* New York: Alfred A. Knopf, 1981.

Malec, James, Russell E. Glasgow, Robert Ely, and John Kling. "Coping with Pain: A Self-Management Approach." *Journal Supplement Abstract Service Pamphlet.* Arlington, Virginia: American Psychological Association, 1977.

Manaster, Guy J., and Raymond J. Corsini. *Individual Psychology.* Itasca, Illinois: F. E. Peacock Publishers, Inc., 1982.

Marin, Peter. "The New Narcissism." *Harper's* (October 1975), pp. 45–56.

May, Rollo. *Love and Will.* New York: W. W. Norton, 1969.
———. *The Courage to Create.* New York: W. W. Norton, 1975.

Medical Self-Care, Access to Health Tools. All issues.

Miller, Alice. *Prisoners of Childhood.* New York: Basic Books, 1981.

Molter, Haya, and George Bach. *Psychoboom.* Düsseldorf, Germany: Diederichs Verlag, 1977.

Nicholson, Luree, and Laura Torbet. *How to Fight Fair with Your Kids . . . and Win!* New York: Harcourt Brace Jovanovich, 1980.

Novaco, Raymond W. "The Cognitive Regulation of Anger and Stress." Edited by P. L. Kendall and S. D. Hollon. *Cognitive Behavioral Interventions: Theory, Research and Procedures.* New York: Academic Press.

Offitt, Avid. *Night Thoughts: Reflections of a Sex Therapist.* New York: Congdon and Lattès, Inc., 1981.

Piaget, Gerald W., and Barbara J. Binkley. *Overcoming Your Barriers: How to Debut and Reprogram Your Personal Biocomputer.* Portola Valley, California, 1981 (published by the authors).

Pines, Maya. "New Focus on Narcissism Offers Analysts Insight into Grandiosity and Emptiness." *The New York Times* (March 16, 1982), p. C1.

Restak, Richard. *The Self Seekers.* New York: Doubleday, 1982.

Rubenstein, Carin. "The Revolution Within" ("Field Report" feature). *Psychology Today* (August 1981), pp. 78–81.

Sale, Kirkpatrick. *Human Scale.* New York: Coward, McCann, and Geoghegan, 1980.

Schur, Edwin. *The Awareness Trap: Self-Absorption Instead of Social Change.* New York: McGraw-Hill, 1977.

Shaver, Phillip, Wyndol Furman, Duane Buhrmester, and Tish Williams. "State into Trait Loneliness During the Transition into College," presented as part of the symposium on New Directions in Loneliness Research at the American Psychological Association Convention, Los Angeles, California, August 28, 1981.

———, and Carin Rubenstein. "Childhood Attachment Experience and Adult Loneliness." *Review of Personality and Social Psychology,* Vol. 1. Beverly Hills, California: Sage, 1980, pp. 42–73.

Singer, Dorothy G., and Tracey A. Revenson. *A Piaget Primer: How a Child Thinks.* New York: New American Library (A Plume Book), 1978.

Stoller, Robert J. *Sexual Excitement: Dynamics of Erotic Life.* New York: Pantheon, 1979.

Turkington, Carol. "Acute, Chronic Depression Can Double Up." *APA Monitor.* American Psychological Association (February 1982), p. 11.

Ullman, Montague, and Nan Zimmerman. *Working with Dreams.* New York: Delacorte Press/Eleanor Friede, 1979.

Warner, Samuel J. *Self-Realizations and Self-Defeat.* New York: Grove Press, Inc., 1967.

Williams, Tennessee. *The Glass Menagerie.* New York: New Directions, 1970.

Winnicott, D. W. "The Maturational Process and the Facilitating Environment." *Studies in the Theory of Emotional Development.* New York: International Universities Press, Inc., 1965.

Wright, Elliott. *Holy Company: Christian Heroes and Heroines.* New York: Macmillan, Inc., 1981.

Yankelovich, Daniel. *New Rules: Searching for Self-Fulfillment in a World Turned Upside Down.* New York: Random House, 1981.

Index